Coins

Coins
and
Crosses

Understanding the Role of Money in the Secular and the Spiritual

Mark DiGiovanni

Other Books by Mark DiGiovanni

TABLE OF CONTENTS

Dedicated to those
who keep the Faith,
whatever their Faith may be.

PREFACE

sec-u-lar - *adj.* **1**. Worldly rather than spiritual. **2.** Not specifically pertaining to religion or to a religious body.

spir-i-tu-al – *adj.* **1.** Of, relating to, consisting of, or having the nature of spirit; not tangible or material. **2.** Of, concerned with, or affecting the soul. **3.** Of, from, or pertaining to God; deific.

(Above definitions from *The American Heritage Dictionary*, second college edition)

Let's make sure we're on the same page, beginning with this first page.

As a beginning, it's important to realize that the secular and the spiritual are not enemy combatants. *Secularity* is the state of being separate from religion, or not being exclusively allied with or against any particular religion. Governments at all levels in the U.S. are secular, yet the government provides tax-exempt status to religious organizations, and the federal government even imprints "In God We Trust" on all our currency.

The secular world is quite capable of coexisting with and even enabling spirituality. To be secular simply means that no particular religion receives preferential treatment. Those whose particular religion comprises the majority may find such neutrality vexing, but neutrality helps assure that one's religion will not be subject to different treatment by secular society should they one day lose that majority. As the first amendment to the U.S. Constitution clearly states, "Congress shall make no law respecting an establishment of religion, or prohibiting the free exercise thereof."

Secular is the easier term to define because it's defined by what it isn't – specifically, religious or spiritual in nature. Historically, the words *religious* and *spiritual* have been used synonymously to describe all the various aspects of the concept of religion. While virtually all religions focus on our spiritual nature, one need not be religious to be spiritual. Approximately one in four Americans proclaim themselves to be "spiritual but not religious". For our discussion, I will assume that all those who consider themselves religious also consider themselves to be spiritual and that those who consider themselves to be spiritual do not necessarily consider themselves to be religious. In other words, for our purposes, religious is a subset of spiritual.

Those who seek to become more spiritual often feel the best way to become so is to transcend the secular. They feel that in order to reach up to the divine, they must first push away from the terrestrial. Monasticism is a religious way of life in which one renounces worldly pursuits to devote oneself fully to spiritual work. Few of us have the option of joining a monastery, so we have to find a way to become more spiritual while immersed in a secular world.

The secular and the spiritual are not mutually exclusive, either. *Secular spirituality* refers to the adherence to a spiritual ideology without advocating a religious framework. Secular spirituality may embrace many of the same types of practices as religious spirituality. Secular spirituality centers on the inner peace of the individual rather than on a relationship with the divine. Proponents advocate forms of secular spirituality in which the motivation is to live happily and/or to help others. Secular spirituality emphasizes humanistic qualities such as love, compassion, patience, forgiveness, responsibility, harmony, and a concern for others.

The term "secularism" was first coined by British writer George Jacob Holyoake in 1851 to describe a social order separate from religion. In his own words, Holyoake argued,

> *"Secularism is not an argument against Christianity; it is one independent of it. It does not question the pretensions of Christianity; it advances others. Secularism does not say there is no light or guidance elsewhere, but maintains that there is light and guidance in secular truth, whose conditions and sanctions exist independently, and act forever. Secular knowledge is manifestly that kind of knowledge which is founded in this life, which relates to the conduct of this life, conduces to the welfare of this life, and is capable of being tested by the experience of this life."*

Secularism, as defined and discussed in this book, is not and should not be equated with atheism (or Socialism, Nazism, or any other 'isms', for that matter). Spiritualism, as defined and discussed in this book, should not be equated with religious fundamentalism of any stripe. I'm presuming that all readers of this book are looking for new insights, which requires an open mind. Anyone looking for ammunition to support a particular agenda, on the right or the left, isn't likely to find it here.

Even though money is a secular creation, no other secular creation has had a greater effect on the world of religion and spirituality than money. And perhaps no greater example exists of money's effect on the spiritual than the selling of indulgences.

According to the teachings outlined in the Catechism of the Catholic Church, two distinct types of consequences follow when a person sins: eternal and temporal. A mortal sin (one that's grave or serious in nature and is committed knowingly and freely) is equivalent to rejecting God and communion with Him. The loss of eternal life with God and the eternal death of Hell is the effect of this rejection. In addition to this eternal punishment due to mortal sin, every sin, including venial sin, is a turning away from God through what the Catechism of the Catholic Church calls an unhealthy attachment to creatures, an attachment that must be purified either here on earth or after death in the state called Purgatory.

In this life, the necessary cleansing from sin can be achieved, at least in part, through prayer, penance, and works of mercy and charity. The Catholic doctrine of the communion of saints teaches that the work of cleansing or sanctification doesn't have to be done entirely by the sinner directly; it's possible for others to accept the burden of answering for the sinner's sins.

In Catholic theology, an *indulgence* is technically a remission of the temporal punishment which would have been inflicted for a previously forgiven sin as a natural consequence of having sinned. An indulgence thus does not forgive the guilt of sin, nor does it repeal the eternal punishment for unforgiven mortal sins. It's not a permit to commit sin, a pardon of future sin, nor a guarantee of salvation for oneself or for another. Ordinarily, forgiveness of mortal sins is obtained through Confession.

The earliest record of a plenary indulgence was Pope Urban II's declaration at the Council of Clermont in 1095, where he remitted all penance incurred by crusaders who had confessed their sins in the Sacrament of Penance, considering participation in the Crusades equivalent to a complete penance.

Indulgences became increasingly popular in the Middle Ages as a reward for displaying piety and doing good deeds. Good deeds included charitable donations of money for a good cause. Building projects funded by indulgences included churches, hospitals, leper colonies, schools, roads, and bridges.

However, the later Middle Ages saw the growth of considerable abuses. Greedy commissaries sought to extract the maximum amount of money for each indulgence. Professional "pardoners", who were sent to collect alms for a specific project, practiced the unrestricted sale of indulgences. Many of these pardoners promised rewards like salvation from eternal damnation in return for money. Indulgences also became a way for Catholic rulers to fund expensive projects, such as Crusades and cathedrals, by keeping a significant portion of the money raised from indulgences in their lands. There was a tendency to forge documents declaring that indulgences had been granted. Indulgences grew to extraordinary magnitude in terms of longevity and breadth of forgiveness.

The scandalous conduct of the pardoners was a catalyst for the Protestant Reformation. In 1517, Pope Leo X offered indulgences for those who gave alms to rebuild St. Peter's Basilica in Rome. The aggressive marketing practices in promoting this cause provoked Martin Luther to write his Ninety-Five Theses, condemning what he saw as the purchase and sale of salvation. The Ninety-Five Theses not only denounced such transactions as worldly, but also denied the Pope's right to grant pardons on God's behalf in the first place. The only thing indulgences guaranteed, Luther said, was an increase in profit and greed because the pardon of the Church was in God's power alone.

The selling of indulgences not only damaged the Catholic Church and led to the Protestant Reformation, those who were able to obtain indulgences felt less constrained in their behavior. They believed they could buy their way out of punishment for their sins and were therefore more inclined toward sin.

Five-hundred years later, we still face many of the same problems where our spiritual lives and money intersect. Money is still the most indispensable tool to avoid punishment for one's sins. The financial crisis of 2008-2009 led to fines for many of the Wall Street firms responsible for the crisis, but no one has gone to jail. Capital punishment's other definition is: if you have the capital, you won't get the punishment.

I Googled "mega church money scandals"; it yielded 322,000 results. The top listing was a story about the founding pastor of the world's largest Pentecostal congregation, located in South Korea, who was sentenced to three years in prison for embezzling $12 million in church funds. Every few months in the U.S., a story breaks about some financial scandal at a church. The typical storyline involves a pastor or other high church official skimming money from the church coffers to support a lavish lifestyle or, more rarely, illegal activities.

Because money is probably mankind's strongest representation of the secular, those who seek to become more spiritual often begin by rejecting money. They may cite as their rationale a quote from the Bible – "Money is the root of all evil."

That quote is from the Bible, but it's incomplete. The actual words are from 1Timothy 6:10:

> *For the love of money is the root of all evil. Some people, eager for money, have wandered from the faith and pierced themselves with many griefs.*

This particular Bible verse is a great example of how words can be misinterpreted when they're segmented or taken out of context. Money isn't the root of all evil – the <u>love</u> of money is the root of all evil.

Money is not moral or immoral. Money is *amoral*, which simply means it is neutral. Humans transmit their own morality and immorality, their own virtues and vices, into and through money.

Money is simply one of the many tools invented by humans to accomplish tasks. It may help to think of money in the way you would think of some other tool, like a hammer. A hammer can be used to do wonderful things, like building a house. It can also be used to do terrible things, like bludgeoning a person to death. Whatever the hammer's purpose, no one ever holds the hammer responsible. We don't give the hammer credit for building the house, and we don't charge the hammer with murder. Such recognition or accusation is reserved for the person who wields the tool, not for the tool itself.

Because money is such a powerful tool, it can be tempting to shift some of our responsibilities about money to the money itself. Money's enormous capabilities make it easier for money to become a misused tool and to even have us love it and worship it in a way that should be reserved for God alone.

If money has a bad reputation in some circles because of its ability to bring out the worst in some people, money has the ability to bring out the best in people as well.

Money's enormous versatility and capabilities make it the most indispensable tool for doing good, as well as for doing evil. Stewardship and charity programs typically focus on three areas of giving – time, talent, and treasure. While time and talent are very necessary gifts for any program, their usefulness does have its limits. The talent pool of the people being solicited may simply be inadequate to meet the needs of the soliciting program. Our time always seems to be in short supply, and the only time we can offer is the present moment. Talents are specialized, and time has zero shelf life.

There are times when only money can meet the needs of a spiritual undertaking. Since 1999, I've chaired the finance committee at my Episcopal Church in metropolitan Atlanta, Georgia. I also serve on our stewardship committee. These experiences have helped me learn the limitations of time and talent. The giving of time and talent are very necessary for both the well-being of our church and the well-being of our members. However, there are needs our church has that simply cannot be filled by any amount of time and talent offered.

Like every church, we have monthly utility bills and insurance bills. We use supplies in our office. We require an annual outside audit. All of these expenses, plus dozens of others, have to be paid for every year, and none of them can be paid for with time and talent. The only legal tender to meet these obligations is actual legal tender issued by a secular organization, the U.S.

Government. We may be well-liked by our vendors, but that won't last long if they don't get paid, with money.

As long as a spiritual undertaking has dealings with the secular world, money will be a necessary tool in that undertaking. Even monks, who eschew almost all of the trappings of the secular world, require money to some extent. They attempt to be self-sufficient, but they still have to make products to sell and accept charitable offerings (in money) to purchase what they cannot produce themselves, such as electricity. Remember, the last era that was virtually moneyless had the western world living in much the same way that monks in the twenty-first century live today. That period was known as the Dark Ages.

Our secular and our spiritual worlds each have a place and a purpose in our lives. There are unique aspects to each, but there's considerable overlap as well. The challenge for each of us during our time on this planet is to balance the secular and the spiritual in a way that brings the greatest benefit to ourselves and to others, both in this life and the next one (if you so believe). Money is simply a tool, and a very valuable one, that can enable us to fulfill our missions in both the secular and spiritual realms.

GOD WOULD LIKE A WORD REGARDING MONEY

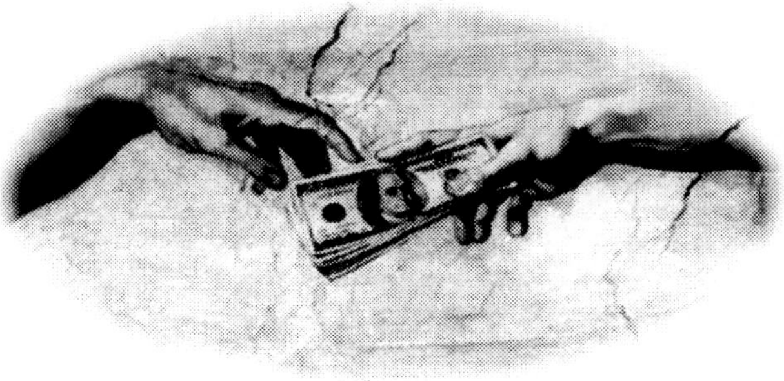

(Apologies to Michelangelo)

The frequency with which money is mentioned in the Bible leads me to two conclusions:

1. God has some definite opinions about money, and
2. God has some serious concerns about mankind's relationship with money.

The Bible isn't the only place where the relationship between God, Man, and money is addressed. All of the major religions speak at length about the intersection of the spiritual and the secular, and they're all quite similar in their perspectives on the subject. We'll look at what Judaism, Islam, Hinduism, and Buddhism say about money shortly.

No matter the money-related topic, there's no shortage of Bible scripture to advise you on that topic.

- **On Budgeting:**

"For which of you, intending to build a tower, does not sit down first and count the cost, whether he may have enough to finish it; lest perhaps, after he has laid the foundation and is not able to finish, all those seeing

begin to mock him, saying, This man began to build and was not able to finish."

- Luke 14:28-30

On the first day of every week each one of you is to put aside and save, as he may prosper, so that no collections be made when I come.

- I Corinthians 16:2

The thoughts of the diligent tend only to plenty; but the thoughts of everyone who is hasty only to poverty.

- Proverbs 21:5

Through wisdom a house is built, and by understanding it is established; and by knowledge the rooms shall be filled with all precious and pleasant riches.

- Proverbs 24:3-4

He who has no rule over his own spirit is like a broken down city without a wall.

- Proverbs 25:28

- **On Debt:**

The Lord will open for you His good storehouse, the heavens, to give rain to your land in its season and to bless all the work of your hand, and you shall lend to many nations, but you shall not borrow.

- Deuteronomy 28:12

The wicked borrows and does not pay back, but the righteous is gracious and gives.

- Psalms 37:21

The rich rules over the poor, and the borrower becomes the lender's slave.

- Proverbs 22:7

Do not be a man who strikes hands in pledge or puts up security for debts; if you lack the means to pay, your very bed will be snatched from under you.

- Proverbs 22:26-27

Owe nothing to anyone except to love one another; for he who loves his neighbor has fulfilled the law.

- Romans 13:8

- **On Getting Rich Quickly:**

He that maketh haste to be rich shall not be innocent.

-Proverbs 28:20

Six days do your work, but on the seventh day do not work, so that your ox and your donkey may rest and the slave born in your household, and the alien as well, may be refreshed.

- Exodus 23:12

Wealth obtained by fraud dwindles, but the one who gathers by labor increases it.

- Proverbs 13:11

- **On Giving**

There is one who scatters, and yet increases all the more, and there is one who withholds what is justly due, and yet it results only in want. The generous man will be prosperous, and he who waters will himself be watered.

- Proverbs 11:24-25

"But when you give to the poor, do not let your left hand know what your right hand is doing, so that your giving will be in secret; and your Father who sees what is done in secret will reward you."

- Matthew 6:3-4

He who gives to the poor will never want, but he who shuts his eyes will have many curses.

- Proverbs 28:27

And He sat down opposite the treasury, and began observing how the people were putting money into the treasury; and many rich people were putting in large sums. A poor widow came and put in two small copper coins, which amount to a cent. Calling His disciples to Him, He said to them, "Truly I say to you, this poor widow put in more than all the contributors to the treasury; for they all put in out of their surplus, but she, out of her poverty, put in all she owned, all she had to live on."

- Mark 12:41-44

As soon as the command was spread abroad, the people of Israel gave in abundance the first fruits of grain, wine, oil, honey, and of all the produce of the field. And they brought in abundantly the tithe of everything.

-II Chronicles 31:5-6

Now this I say, he who sows sparingly will also reap sparingly, and he who sows bountifully will also reap bountifully. Each one must do just as he has purposed in his heart, not grudgingly or under compulsion, for God loves a cheerful giver.

- II Corinthians 9:6-8

- **On Planning:**

Without consultation, plans are frustrated, but with many counselors they succeed.

-Proverbs 15:22

Divide your portion to seven, or even to eight, for you do not know what misfortune may occur on the earth.

- Ecclesiastes 11:2

"Then the kingdom of heaven will be comparable to ten virgins, who took their lamps and went out to meet the bridegroom. Five of them were foolish, and five were

prudent. For when the foolish took their lamps, they took no oil with them, but the prudent took oil in flasks along with their lamps. Now while the bridegroom was delaying, they all got drowsy and began to sleep. But at midnight there was a shout, 'Behold, the bridegroom! Come out to meet him.' Then all those virgins rose and trimmed their lamps. The foolish said to the prudent, 'Give us some of your oil, for our lamps are going out.' But the prudent answered, 'No, there will not be enough for us and you too; go instead to the dealers and buy some for yourselves.' And while they were going away to make the purchase, the bridegroom came, and those who were ready went in with him to the wedding feast; and the door was shut. Later the other virgins also came, saying, 'Lord, lord, open up for us.' But he answered, 'Truly I say to you, I do not know you.' Be on the alert then, for you do not know the day nor the hour."

- Matthew 25:1-13

- **On Work:**

Poor is he who works with a negligent hand, but the hand of the diligent makes rich.

- Proverbs 10:4

He also who is slack in his work is brother to him who destroys.

- Proverbs 18:9

Do you see a man skilled in his work? He will stand before kings; he will not stand before obscure men.

- Proverbs 22:29

For even when we were with you, we used to give you this order: if anyone is not willing to work, then he is not to eat, either. For we hear that some among you are leading an undisciplined life, doing no work at all, but acting like busybodies.

- II Thessalonians 2:9

But if anyone does not provide for his own, and especially for those of his household, he has denied the faith and is worse than an unbeliever.

- I Timothy 5:8

For God is not unjust so as to forget your work and the love which you have shown toward His name, in having ministered and in still ministering to the saints.

- Hebrews 6:10

- **On Priorities:**

"Do not be afraid, little flock, for your Father has been pleased to give you the Kingdom. Sell your possessions and give to the poor. Provide purses for yourself that will not wear out, a treasure in heaven that will not be destroyed, where no thief comes near and no moth destroys. For where your treasure is, there your heart will be also."

- Luke 12:32-34

"He went to him and bandaged his wounds, pouring on oil and wine. Then he put the man on his own donkey, brought him to an inn and took care of him. The next day he took out two denarii and gave them to the innkeeper. 'Look after him,' he said, 'and when I return, I will reimburse you for any extra expense you may have."

- Luke 10:34-35

"For what does it profit a man, to gain the whole world and lose his soul?"

- Mark 8:36

He who is faithful in a very little thing is faithful also in much; and he who is unrighteous in a very little thing is unrighteous also in much.

- Luke 16:10

"Woe to you, scribes and Pharisees, hypocrites! For you tithe mint and dill and cumin, and have neglected the weightier provisions of the law: justice and mercy and faithfulness; but these are the things you should have done without neglecting the others. You blind guides! You strain out a gnat but swallow a camel."

- Matthew 23:23-24

"Render to Caesar the things that are Caesar's; and to God the things that are God's."

- Matthew 22:21

"No one can serve two masters; for either he will hate the one and love the other, or he will be devoted to one and despise the other. You cannot serve God and wealth."

- Matthew 6:24

Remember the Lord your God, for it is He who gives you the ability to produce wealth.

-Deuteronomy 8:18

"From everyone to whom much has been given, much will be required; and from the one to whom much has been entrusted, even more will be demanded."

-Luke 12:42-48

Jesus said to him, "If you wish to be complete, go and sell your possessions and give to the poor, and you will have treasure in heaven; and come, follow Me." But when the young man heard this statement, he went away grieving; for he was one who owned much property. And Jesus said to His disciples, "Truly I say to you, it is hard for a rich man to enter the kingdom of heaven. "Again I say to you, it is easier for a camel to go through the eye of a needle, than for a rich man to enter the kingdom of God." When the disciples heard this, they were very astonished and said, "Then who can be saved?" And looking at them Jesus said to them, "With people this is impossible, but with God all things are possible."

- Matthew 19:21-26

"Do not worry about your life, what you will eat or drink, or about your body, what you will wear. Look at the birds of the air; they do not sow or reap, yet your Heavenly father feeds them."

- Matthew 6:25-26

One of the most well-known sections of the Bible is Exodus 20:1-17, more commonly known as the Ten Commandments. The Ten Commandments are God's minimum expectations for us. The Ten Commandments are cornerstones of Jewish and Christian teachings, but similar rules/guidelines occur in all the major religions.

There are many theories about why there are exactly Ten Commandments. Ten is, of course, the basis of our numbering system, which is based on our number of fingers. In Mel Brooks' movie, *The History of the World, Part 1*, Moses comes down from Mount Sinai with fifteen commandments on three stone tablets. He accidentally drops one and immediately amends the fifteen Commandments to ten.

George Carlin has a bit where he dissects the Ten Commandments and concludes that we really only need two:

> *"Thou shalt always be honest and faithful to the provider of thy nookie, and Thou shalt try real hard not to kill anyone, unless of course they pray to a different invisible man than you. Two is all you*

need. I wouldn't mind folks posting them on the courthouse wall, as long as they provided one additional commandment: Thou shalt keep thy religion to thyself."

The desire to reduce even a small number of commandments is probably just human nature. The fewer rules there are, the less likely we are to break one. Or, as Winston Churchill put it, "If you have ten thousand regulations, you destroy all respect for the law."

The Ten Commandments were given to Moses eight-hundred to a thousand years before King Croesus and the Lydians invented coins and money. Yet, there's a large financial component to at least five and as many as eight of the Ten Commandments. Here's my analysis:

I – THOU SHALT HAVE NO OTHER GODS BEFORE ME and II – THOU SHALT NOT MAKE UNTO THEE ANY GRAVEN IMAGE.
Graven images were typically made of gold, which served as money in ancient times. *Mammon* is defined as riches and, more specifically, the desire for riches. Mammon (aka money) is the number one challenger to God, which Jesus reminds us when He says we can't serve both.

III – THOU SHALT NOT TAKE THE NAME OF THE LORD THY GOD IN VAIN.
There seems to be no financial incentive to break this commandment, so I'll give it a pass.

IV – REMEMBER THE SABBATH DAY TO KEEP IT HOLY.
This commandment serves a practical purpose in that it commands a day of rest. Without a commandment to

abstain from work one day a week, many people would work their livestock, their servants, and themselves to an early death.

V. HONOR THY FATHER AND THY MOTHER.
With people living longer, while the cost of care for the elderly continues to soar, this commandment has even more financial relevance now than in Moses' time.

VI. THOU SHALT NOT KILL.
Throughout history, wars have most frequently begun when one group wanted some kind of wealth another group possessed. Besides love (or some demented form of it), money has historically been the biggest motivation to commit murder.

VII. THOU SHALT NOT COMMIT ADULTERY.
This is the other commandment that has little financial incentive to commit. Committing it can, however, incur a serious financial penalty.

VIII. THOU SHALT NOT STEAL.
No analysis needed here.

IX. THOU SHALT NOT BEAR FALSE WITNESS AGAINST THY NEIGHBOR.
Lying for financial gain is as old as the human race, and we aren't above lying about others for those gains. Perjury committed in a civil suit is a perfect example of breaking this commandment for financial gain.

X. THOU SHALT NOT COVET.
Coveting someone's possessions is not only triggered by wealth disparity, coveting is also a leading cause in the violation of commandments VI, VII, VIII, and IX.

The *Torah* (Hebrew for teaching or instruction) consists of what Christians refer to as the first five books of the Old Testament – Genesis, Exodus, Leviticus, Numbers, and Deuteronomy. The Torah is part of the *Tanakh,* also referred to as the Hebrew Bible. In addition to the Torah, the Tanakh also contains two other categories: the *Nevi'im* (Hebrew for Prophets), which includes the books of Joshua, Judges, Samuel, Kings, Isaiah, Jeremiah, Ezekiel, Hosea, Joel, Amos, Obadiah, Jonah, Micah, Nahum, Habakkuk, Zephaniah, Haggai, Zachariah, and Malachi; the *Ketuvim* (Hebrew for writings) which includes the books of Psalms, Proverbs, Job, Song of Songs, Ruth, Lamentations, Ecclesiastes, Esther, Daniel, Ezra, Nehemiah, and Chronicles.

Unlike the classical Christian view, Judaism sees no virtue in poverty. Poverty is viewed as pointless suffering, and the test of wealth is viewed as great as or greater than the test of poverty.

Because poverty is something to be avoided, Jews are exhorted to earn their living through gainful employment. Jewish law calls upon Jews to do everything in their power to avoid becoming a burden to others. They're to be responsible for their own welfare and not rely on the community to provide for them. Although the wealthy are called upon to be charitable to the poor, this doesn't absolve the poor from their responsibility to earn a living.

Tzedakah is a Hebrew word literally meaning justice or righteousness, but commonly used to signify charity. It's a somewhat different concept than charity because tzedakah is an obligation, while charity is typically understood as a spontaneous act of goodwill and a marker of generosity.

While the second highest form of tzedakah is to give donations anonymously to unknown recipients, the highest form is to give a gift, loan, or partnership that will result in the recipient supporting himself instead of living upon others. Unlike philanthropy or charity, which is completely voluntary, tzedakah is seen as a religious obligation, which must be performed regardless of financial standing and must even be performed by the poor. Tzedakah is considered to be one of the three main acts that can amend a less than favorable heavenly decree.

In Judaism, a fifth of one's income is considered a generous contribution to charity and shouldn't be exceeded. It's forbidden to become impoverished by distributing all of one's wealth to charity, and one who does so is considered foolishly pious. However, one may leave as much as one-third of his estate to charity in his will.

A minimum of one-tenth of one's income (*tithe* means one-tenth of income or production) belongs to God and should be used for charity or other religious purposes. If there's an urgent need for charity or to perform any other commandment, one must sacrifice a fifth, or at least a tenth, of all his possessions. After the first time, however, one need only tithe from his yearly income. In any case, the very wealthy should give as much as is needed.

One of the principles of *Islam* is that all things belong to God and that wealth is therefore held by humans in trust. This principle parallels the Christian belief that we're merely stewards of what belongs to God.

One of the five pillars of Islam is *zakat*, which concerns the giving of one's money and/or goods. Zakat means both purification and growth. Muslims often believe that giving through the zakat will purify them of sin and that God uses it as a test of true Islamic belief. The zakat consists of annually giving 2.5 per cent of one's goods or funds.

Zakat is based on giving a percentage of one's net wealth, whereas tithing is based on giving a percentage of one's income. Zakat may actually be a more equitable standard for giving than tithing because it focuses on wealth rather than income. For example, one person has an income of $40,000 and a net worth of $30,000. (The lower the income, the harder it is to build wealth.) Another person has an income of $150,000 and a net worth of $1,000,000. For the first person, the annual standard of giving is $4,000 under the tithe and $750 under zakat. For the second person, the standard is $15,000 under the tithe and $25,000 under zakat.

Muslims generally associate the zakat with specifically giving to the poor. According to the Quran, there are eight categories of people who qualify to receive zakat funds:

1. Those living in absolute poverty
2. Those restrained because they can't meet their basic needs
3. The zakat collectors themselves
4. Non-Muslims who are sympathetic to Islam or wish to convert to Islam
5. People whom one is attempting to free from slavery or bondage (also includes paying ransom or blood money)
6. Those who've incurred overwhelming debts while attempting to satisfy their basic needs
7. Those working in God's way
8. Children of the street and travelers.

Zakat is meant to discourage the hoarding of capital and to stimulate investment. Because the individual must pay zakat on the net wealth, wealthy Muslims are compelled to invest in profitable ventures, or otherwise see their wealth slowly erode. Furthermore, means of production such as equipment, factories, and tools are exempt from zakat, which further provides the incentive to invest wealth in productive businesses.

The Quran talks about the zakat in more than 30 different verses. In the Quranic view, zakat is a way to redistribute wealth, thus defining a charity-based economy with a particular interest in the poor and dispossessed Muslims. Zakat is considered more than taxation. One must give zakat for the sake of one's salvation: while those who give zakat can expect reward from God in the afterlife, neglecting to give zakat can result in damnation. The giving of the zakat is considered a means of purifying one's wealth and soul.

There are five principles that should be followed when giving the zakat:

1. The giver must declare to God his intention to give the zakat.
2. The zakat must be paid on the day it's due.
3. After the offering, the payer must not exaggerate on spending his money.
4. Payment must be in kind. The wealthy should pay a portion of their income. Those who don't have much money should compensate for it in different ways, such as good deeds and good behavior toward others.
5. The zakat must be distributed in the community from which it was taken.

Islam encourages man to utilize, to the fullest possible sense and responsibly, all the resources that God has created and entrusted to man for his use. Non-utilization of these resources for his benefit and for that of the society is tantamount to ungratefulness to God, as is irresponsibility and extravagance. Wealth is considered an important means by which man can pave the way for the attainment of his ultimate objective. Islam refers to wealth as "good", an object of delight and pleasure, and a support for the community. Conversely, involuntary poverty is considered as undesirable.

The earning of wealth is qualified through emphasizing that wealth is only a means for the achievement of man's ultimate objective and not an end in itself. It must be earned through good, productive, and beneficial work. Unlawfully acquired or accumulated wealth for its own sake is condemned as corruption.

Islam considers wealth as the life-blood of the community which must be constantly in circulation; therefore, its possession excludes the right of hoarding (Quran 9:34-35). The implication is that lawfully earned wealth must be invested within the community to improve its economic well-being. Investing wealth is not only measured by the monetary gain associated with it, but also by the benefit which accrues to the society. The needs of the society, therefore, must be a consideration for the owner of wealth.

Islam teaches that when one spends his wealth in the way of God, there's no decrease in wealth. One's wealth actually increases as it's given away; God replaces it with something better and greater. "The example of those who spend their wealth in the way of God is like a seed of grain which grows seven spikes; in each spike is a hundred grains. And God multiplies His reward for whom He wills." (Quran 2:261).

In *Hinduism*, the world's oldest religion, wealth is considered divine and an essential requirement for the preservation and continuation of life on earth. God is the source of all wealth and abundance. *Lakshmi* is the goddess of good fortune and prosperity and is revered by Hindus.

In Hinduism, there isn't just one purpose of human life, but four, the first two of which are relevant to our discussion:

1. Dharma - fulfilling one's purpose
2. Artha - prosperity
3. Kama - desire, sexuality, enjoyment
4. Moksha - enlightenment

The Sanskrit word *dharma* has many meanings, including law, teaching, and religion. In this context, it means one's destiny or purpose. In general, it refers to one's vocation or career, which is often defined by class and family. Dharma also means righteousness, or living morally and ethically at all times.

Another aspect of dharma is paying the *five debts*. Hindus believe that they're born in debt to the gods and various humans and that they must repay those karmic debts during their lifetime. The debts are:

1. Debt to the gods for their blessings; paid by rituals and offerings
2. Debt to parents and teachers; paid by supporting them, having children of one's own and passing along knowledge
3. Debt to guests; repaid by treating them as if they were gods visiting one's home
4. Debt to other human beings; repaid by treating them with respect
5. Debt to all other living beings; repaid by offering good will, food or any other help that's appropriate.

Artha is prosperity or success in worldly pursuits. Although the ultimate goal of Hinduism is enlightenment, the pursuit of wealth and prosperity is regarded as an appropriate pursuit for the householder. Artha also ensures social order, since there would be no society if everyone renounced worldly life to meditate. But while Hindus are encouraged to make money, it must be within the bounds of dharma.

It's acceptable for Hindus to pray for money, and at *Divali* (Festival of Light) many Hindu business people make offerings to Lakshmi, asking her to make them prosperous. This practice doesn't mean Hindus believe greed to be acceptable. Money is seen as necessary, but it shouldn't be seen as the most important thing.

There are ten *Niyamas* (observances or practices) in Hinduism:

1. *Hri* – being modest and showing remorse for misdeeds
2. *Santosha* – seeking contentment and joy in life
3. *Dana* – giving or charity
4. *Astikya* – Faith in God(s)
5. *Ishvarapujana* – cultivating devotion though daily worship and meditation
6. *Siddhanta Sravana* – studying the teachings and listening to the elders
7. *Mati* – developing a spiritual will and intellect
8. *Vrata* – faithfully fulfilling religious rules, vows, and observances
9. *Japa* – chanting mantras daily
10. *Tapas* – practicing austerity, penance, sacrifice

Number 3, dana, is the Niyama concerned with money. A question that's often asked about offering dana is, "How much should I give?" Unlike the practices of tithing and zakat, dana doesn't have strict guidelines or percentage amounts that people should give. The following are recommended starting points in finding the balance between giving too little and giving too much:

- There's no fixed or recommended amount, as the dharma is priceless. It's a personal decision.
- This decision should be based on your current financial means.
- See how you feel when you're making an offering. If making the offering makes you feel anxious, rather than happy, you may be stretching your ability to give too far, or perhaps you're holding on too tightly to whatever you're giving.
- Look at your motivation. Are you giving out of pure kindness or out of wanting something in return?

Buddhism actually began as a protest against the egregious elements of the Hindu society, including the brutality of the caste system. In essence, it was a reform movement that grew out of the corruption and restrictive power structure of Hinduism. The relationship between the two can be likened to that between Catholicism and Protestantism.

It's a widely held view that the Buddha taught his followers to turn away from the secular world and seek happiness in a life of renunciation. While this view isn't wrong, it turns out to be an incomplete picture.

The Buddha advised his lay followers to lead happy and productive lives. Far from disdaining the worldly life, the Buddha suggested that his followers engage with it fully and wholeheartedly and taught that it's a genuine source of happiness.

Buddhism's teachings on renunciation were specifically intended for the monastic community, though he certainly spoke of a higher bliss that could be found in a renounced life. "Happiness in detachment" is a more stable form of happiness because it comes from within and isn't dependent on unreliable things like wealth, relationships, or social status.

But the Buddha understood that the renounced lifestyle isn't for everyone. And he never intended those teachings to apply to everyone.

Buddhism's view on prosperity can be summarized as follows:

- One is entitled to as much wealth as one wants, as long as it's earned ethically, without harming others. We're told to "gradually increase wealth without squeezing others, just as bees collect honey without harming the flowers."
- We need to use our wealth to benefit both ourselves and others. In other words, wealth isn't to be pursued for its own sake, but for the good it can do for the world.
- We need to be good citizens – we should pay taxes to our government and also support the monks and other spiritual leaders who have dedicated their lives to the benefit of all.
- We need to be moderate in our way of satisfying our senses. It's fine to enjoy good food or fine clothing, for example, as long as we don't get greedy or overindulge.

Buddhism professes that there are four kinds of happiness derived from wealth. They are:

1. *Atthisukha* - the happiness of ownership
2. *Anavajjasukha* - the happiness derived from wealth which is earned by means of a right livelihood, one that isn't harmful to others
3. *Ananasukha* - the happiness derived from being debt-free

4. *Bhogasukha* - the happiness of sharing one's wealth. This kind of happiness is an extremely important concept in Buddhism.

Although the Buddha saw that economic stability was important for man's happiness, he also saw the harmful side of wealth. He saw that man's natural desires are such that wealth provides ample opportunity for these desires to be indulged.

The Buddha says there are three types of persons to be found in the world: the totally blind, the one who can see with one eye, and, the one who can see with both eyes. The one who is totally blind can neither acquire wealth nor discern right from wrong. The one who can see with one eye can acquire wealth but cannot discern right from wrong. The one who has perfect sight in both eyes is the ideal individual. He can acquire wealth and also discern right from wrong. The Buddhist view is that the ideal man is the one who is wealthy and virtuous.

Dana is practiced in both Buddhism and Hinduism, and both view dana as the cultivation of generosity.

The religions discussed above are practiced by nearly 80% of the world's population. Of the remainder, approximately half are not religious and half practice some other religion, which is usually based on tribe or ethnic group.

Despite the fact that these major religions developed in vastly different parts of the world over vastly different periods of time, there's a surprising consensus about their views on money. This consensus should probably not be surprising, as human behavior has proven to be surprisingly consistent around the world and across time. Our consistent human weaknesses when it comes to money are the main reason for the consistent messages from religions when it comes to our relationship with money.

Here are some of the areas of consensus from these religions when it comes to money. Despite your belief system (or lack thereof), these points are hard to deny:

- Money is a very important tool for achieving our spiritual as well as our earthly goals.
- Money and all other worldly goods have been entrusted to us; we're all stewards.
- Wealth isn't evil per se, but the pursuit of wealth at the price of our integrity definitely is.
- Regardless of our position, we have an obligation to help others.
- Money can play an important role in meeting our obligation to help others.
- Generosity is rewarded, not punished. When we give more, we're given more.
- We're expected to work and to give to our potential; there are consequences for failing to do so.
- An obsession with wealth is one of the biggest impediments to a healthy relationship with our fellow man and with God.

An upcoming chapter takes a look at human behavior, especially when it comes to money. When we understand how we think, feel, and act when it comes to money, we can better understand God's concerns in this area. We can also begin to understand how we can move toward behaviors that can reconcile our relationship with money and our relationship with God.

FROM BEADS TO BYTES – THE EVOLUTION OF MONEY

Lydian coin circa 550 B.C.

Croesus (pronounced CREE-suss) was the King of Lydia from 560 to 546 B.C. Lydia was a small kingdom in what is today western Turkey. While the Lydians were known for producing perfume and cosmetics, that wasn't their source of greatness.

While various forms of money were developed fairly simultaneously in different societies, Croesus is credited with the production of the first gold and silver coins to be used in trade; in essence, he invented money as we've known it for over 2,500 years. The widespread use of coins as a medium of exchange enabled Lydia to become the first society to become wealthy from trade and not from conquest. The durability of coins enabled wealth to be accumulated for future use in a way that commodities like grain and cattle could not. The desirability and familiarity of gold and silver to the world at large enabled coins minted from these metals to be accepted as a unit of account and as a medium of exchange by almost everyone, everywhere.

Other cultures had come up with methods of facilitating trade before Croesus, but they had severe limitations. For example, the ancient Aztecs used cacao (from which chocolate is made) to make up the difference when a barter transaction wasn't even. Commodity money like cacao made more trading possible, and commodity money like cacao, tobacco, or deerskins (the original *buck*) had uses all on their own. But such commodities had a limited shelf life, and they were not always accepted in trade.

Because salt is so necessary to life, it had been used as a form of money throughout history. The word salary is derived from the Latin *sal*, meaning salt. Roman soldiers were often paid in salt, and a soldier who did his job well was said to be "worth his salt".

While salt is vital, cacao is tasty, and buckskin is useful, metal is the most practical substance for money. Because it's long-lasting, it's a good store of value. Metal can also be converted into something useful and still retain its value, due to the value of the metal itself.

For the first thousand years of money's history, money was synonymous with coins. Precious metals, in weighed quantities, were a common form of money in ancient times. The transition to quantities that could be counted rather than weighed came gradually. One of the reasons for the rapid spread of the use of coins was their convenience. In situations where coins were generally acceptable at their nominal value, there was no need to weigh them and, in everyday transactions where relatively small numbers were involved, counting was quicker and far more convenient than weighing. By the Middle Ages, monarchs were able to use this convenience as a source of profit by ordering recoinages, enabling them to pocket the difference between a coin's nominal value and its metallic value.

The Roman Empire was actually organized around money. Prior empires favored government as the center of organization, but the Romans realized they could extend their empire further, incorporate conquered peoples into the Roman mindset, and facilitate trade within all parts of the empire with a standardized monetary system. It's said that the coins used to flow from the Roman mint in a constant stream. The Latin word *currere*, which means to flow, was used to describe the stream. Our word *currency* comes from it.

The Roman emperors made extensive use of coins for propaganda; one historian went so far as to claim that "the primary function of the coins is to record the messages which the emperor and his advisers desired to commend to the populations of the empire." Coins were the best propaganda weapon available for advertising Greek, Roman, or any other civilization in the days before mechanical printing was invented. The only way to avoid the propaganda was to avoid the use of money. Atheists could argue that American money today serves a similar purpose with the phrase "In God We Trust" imprinted on every coin and bill issued.

This first generation of money that began with the invention of coins in Lydia more than 2,500 years ago resulted in the first system of open and free markets. After the collapse of the Roman Empire around 476 A.D., the classical money economy that had been in existence for nearly a thousand years collapsed. It would be almost another thousand years before money again became a prominent force in people's lives with the Renaissance and the development of the Italian banking system. The period from the fifth to the fifteenth centuries, when money was virtually non-existent, was, not coincidentally, known as the Dark Ages.

In religious history, probably the most familiar reference to ancient money is in Jesus' Parable of the Talents. In the parable, the master entrusts three servants with five, three, and one talent, respectively. These do not seem like large sums until you realize the actual value of a talent.

A talent was a large silver or gold disk that weighed 75-80 pounds, or about 35 kilograms. One talent was equal to 6,000 drachma. The daily wage for the average worker in the time of Jesus was one drachma, so one talent was roughly equivalent to twenty years' wages. Assuming the average daily wage at that time was equivalent to $15 per hour today, one talent was worth approximately $750,000 in today's dollars. Being a steward of even one talent was a huge responsibility. Such responsibility was not handed out lightly, and failing to meet that responsibility was not treated lightly either, as the Parable of the Talents makes clear.

The invention of banking actually preceded that of coinage. Banking originated in Ancient Mesopotamia, where the royal palaces and temples provided secure places for the safe-keeping of grain and other commodities. Receipts came to be used for transfers not only to the original depositors but also to third parties.

The Crusades gave a great stimulus to banking because payments for supplies, equipment, allies, ransoms etc. required safe and speedy means of transferring vast resources of cash. Consequently, the

Knights of the Temple and the Knights Hospitaller began to provide some banking services, such as those already being developed in some of the Italian city states.

Many societies throughout history have had laws requiring compensation in some form for crimes of violence, an attempt to improve on the Old Testament approach of "an eye for an eye". The word to *pay* is derived from the Latin *pacare,* meaning originally to pacify, appease, or make peace with another through the appropriate unit of value customarily acceptable to both sides. A similarly widespread custom was payment for brides in order to compensate the head of the family for the loss of a daughter's services. Since very ancient times rulers have imposed taxes on or exacted tribute from their subjects. Religious obligations might also entail payment of tribute or sacrifices of some kind. Thus, in many societies there was a requirement for a means of payment for blood-money, bride-money, tax, or tribute, and this gave a great impetus to the spread of money.

In China the issue of paper money became common from about AD 960 onwards, but there had been occasional issues long before that. A motive for one such early issue, in the reign of Emperor Hien Tsung 806-821, was a shortage of copper for making coins. A drain of currency from China, partly to buy off potential invaders from the north, led to greater reliance on paper money, with the result that by 1020 the quantity issued had become excessive, causing inflation. In subsequent centuries there were several episodes of hyperinflation, and after about 1455, after well over 500 years of using paper money, China abandoned it.

With the revival of banking in Western Europe, stimulated by the Crusades in the twelfth and thirteenth centuries, written instructions in the form of bills of exchange came to be used as a means of transferring large sums of money. It's speculated that the Arabs may have used bills of exchange even earlier, perhaps starting in the eighth century. The use of paper as currency came much later.

The second generation of money extended from the beginning of the Renaissance through the Industrial Revolution. It originated in the banks of Italy and eventually created a system of national banks and paper money. The second generation of money destroyed feudalism and changed the basis of economic power from owning land to owning stocks, bonds, and corporations. The third generation that is just now underway is the era of electronic money and the virtual economy.

Even though banking truly came of age during the Italian Renaissance, it garnered little respect at that time. Viewed as moneychangers and as barely disguised moneylenders (usury – the charging of interest on loans - was still forbidden by the church at that time), bankers were viewed only slightly better than pimps and other lowlife criminal types. Possession of wealth had practical importance, but little prestige in the aristocratic systems of Europe.

Up until the last hundred years or so, common people only borrowed money out of desperation. To charge interest on loaned money was the sin of usury, and the Christian Church had strict laws forbidding it. What little money lending there was at the time was often handled by Jews, who were not subject to the constraints of the church. But the laws against usury applied to loans; if some other method, like a contract was used to transfer money, the restrictions on usury could be bypassed without risking excommunication. Around 1300, some clever Italian merchants figured out this loophole.

In the early fourteenth century, the church's power was in decline, and no state powers could yet fill the vacuum. The Knights Templar had been the de facto bankers of Europe with endorsement by the Pope until King Philip IV of France crushed them to obtain their wealth in 1314.

A handful of wealthy families in northern Italy stepped in to fill the void left by the destruction of the Knights Templar. These families had a slightly different business model than the knights. These new financiers served everyone, not just the nobility. And they weren't doing it for God; they were doing it for profit.

The word *bank* is derived from the Italian for *bench*, and these families started modestly by operating from a bench or table at fairs in their hometowns. To avoid accusations of usury from charging interest on a loan, the Italian merchants created and traded bills of exchange, which were written documents that ordered a specific payment in gold or silver to a specific person at a specific place and time. The person writing the bill of exchange acted as an intermediary between someone needing money and someone with the means to provide it, and they collected a fee for their services.

Bills of exchange were a boon to finance. They were much easier to transport than comparable amounts of gold or silver. If a bill of exchange were lost or stolen, it could not be redeemed by another. They were harder to counterfeit than coins because only literates could counterfeit a bill of exchange, and literates were few and far between and occupied the uppermost rungs of society.

Bills of exchange had the effect of increasing the amount of money in circulation, as well as the speed of circulation. Money was now liberated from the physical limitations imposed by scarce and cumbersome coins and a primitive transportation system. The checks and paper money we use today are the descendants of these early bills of exchange.

Even though bills of exchange greatly improved the circulation of money, they ultimately had to be paid in precious metal. The amount of money in circulation, and the ability of an economy to grow were dependent on the amount of gold and silver. This constant need for more gold and silver was the reason for the discovery and colonization of the Americas. Between 1500 and 1800, an estimated 2,800 tons of gold and 155,000 tons of silver were extracted and shipped from Spanish and Portuguese colonies in the Americas to Europe. Because of this influx of gold and silver, money was being produced faster than were goods to buy, leading to Europe's first inflationary economies.

The Spanish and Portuguese colonized what we know as Latin America for the expressed purpose of extracting precious metals. The English and French colonized North America for the purpose of production of a variety of goods. Extraction created money but nothing to buy, leading to inflation. Production created goods without increasing the money supply, making inflation all but impossible.

As economies grew in size and complexity, so did governments. These governments, whether Chinese, Italian, American, or other, saw the issuance of paper money as a way of gaining greater control of the money supply and of their economy. Paper money, as we think of it today, was the creation of Benjamin Franklin who was, among other things, a printer. The success of the American Revolution (as well as the subsequent success of America itself) was made possible by paper money. It was the first war financed in such a manner. Of course, the paper money was, in effect, deficit spending and created horrible inflation during the American Revolution and immediately after. Americans were so disgusted with the economic effects of paper money (despite the fact that it financed their independence) that paper money would virtually disappear from the American scene until the Civil War.

Although paper money obviously had no intrinsic value, its acceptability originally depended on its being backed by some commodity, normally precious metals. During the Napoleonic Wars, convertibility of Bank of England notes was suspended, and there was some inflation, which worried contemporary observers who were used to stable prices. In accordance with the recommendations of an official inquiry, Britain adopted the gold standard for the pound in 1816. For centuries earlier silver had been the standard of value. The pound was originally an amount of silver weighing one pound.

France and the United States were in favor of a bimetallic standard, and in 1867 an international conference was held in Paris to try and widen the area of common currencies based on coins with standard weights of gold and silver. However, when the various German states merged into a single country in 1871, they chose the gold standard. The Scandinavian countries adopted the gold standard shortly afterwards. France made the switch from bimetallism to gold in 1878, and Japan, which had been on a silver standard, changed in

1897. Finally, in 1900, the United States officially adopted the gold standard.

The United States kept the link to gold, and after World War II the U.S. dollar replaced the pound sterling as the key global currency. Other countries fixed their exchange rates against the dollar, the value of which remained defined in terms of gold. In the early 1970s the system of fixed exchange rates started to break down as a result of growing international inflation, and the United States abandoned the link with gold in 1973.

Economies around the world spent much of the twentieth century extricating themselves from the gold standard so that no major world currency is now backed by gold. The great benefit to this change is that economies are no longer limited in size by the amount of gold their governments hold. The risk is that governments will finance expenditures by simply printing more money, which they find preferable to raising taxes. This practice can lead to inflation, as money in circulation increases faster than goods or services available for purchase.

As long as paper money was redeemable in silver or gold, the amount that could be circulated was limited. Paper money was a very practical incarnation, but it couldn't exist separate from gold or silver backing it without creating problems of inflation and public skepticism about its value. Fiscal conservatives had preferred a gold-only standard because its supply now and in the future was more predictable. People needing a larger and looser money supply, farmers in particular, wanted a bi-metal standard of gold and silver. Farmers borrowed regularly during the production cycle, and more money also meant cheaper money in the form of lower interest rates. This conflict between eastern bankers and western farmers was captured in *The Wizard of Oz*, published in 1900. Dorothy and her companions represent the farmers. The counterfeit wizard represents the eastern bankers. (Dorothy's magical slippers are silver in the book; ruby looked better for a Technicolor movie.)

A nation's currency is only as stable as its government's discipline in issuing it. The Treaty of Versailles that ended World War I required Germany to pay reparations totaling some $33 billion, or twice the total annual GDP of the country. As Germany printed more and more money to meet reparation payments, inflation raged. What had cost one German mark at war's end cost 700 billion marks four years later. The chaos and humiliation this hyperinflation created in Germany was a major catalyst for Hitler's rise to power a few years later.

During communist rule in Romania, cigarettes were the currency of choice, much as they are in prisons. If money becomes worthless because the government prints too much of it (post WWI Germany), or if the money is useless because there's nothing to buy (Romania), or if a commodity like cigarettes is a more useful medium of exchange (prisons), then traditional money loses its influence. But these are the exceptions. Money exists simply because it's more useful than the alternatives.

More recently, Zimbabwe's disastrous land reform program has had similar results to Germany after World War I. Over a six-month period in 2008, a loaf of bread went from 200,000 to 1,600,000,000,000 (1.6 trillion) Zimbabwean dollars, an inflation rate of 11,000,000%. When such hyperinflation occurs, money becomes useless as a medium of exchange because it's useless as a store of value. Nations in the grip of such hyperinflation revert to a barter economy or adopt another nation's currency out of necessity.

Money has connected humans in greater numbers than anything before or since its creation. Although the breadth of relationships widened because of money, the depth of relationships narrowed. Money weakened connections that had been based on family, tribe, religion, and nationality. Money enabled the establishment of the bottom line, and the bottom line began to dominate more and more human actions. Money became the measure of the value of work, of time, and even of human life itself. Slaves were first brought to the new world to work the mines to fill the coffers of the European powers with gold and silver.

Money has also been a great democratizing force in history. The ancient Greeks were one of history's greatest cultures, but they didn't have great armies; they couldn't even organize into a single state. Greece became great because of trade made possible by money, which they copied from the Lydians. Money helped the Greeks democratize and made possible a society that could produce people like Plato and Aristotle. Even the word *economics* comes from Greek and means skilled in managing an estate. Money enabled Greek society to more fully tap its potential.

Political freedom and economic strength have moved in tandem throughout history. Prior to the Industrial Revolution, almost no one had a say in selecting their leaders. Today, almost three-quarters of the world's nations are democracies. Not coincidentally, since the Industrial Revolution, the world's wealth has been increasing a hundred times faster than it did before the

Industrial Revolution, and it increases fastest in the most democratic societies.

Money has continuously become less constrained over time. First, it no longer had to be in the form of gold or silver coins. Then, it no longer had to even be backed by gold or silver. The break with precious metals helped to make money a more elusive entity.

Another trend in the same direction is the growing forms of electronic money from the 1990s onward. In some ways e-money is a logical evolution from the wire transfers that came about with the widespread adoption of the telegraph in the nineteenth century, though such transfers had relatively little impact on the everyday shopper. Credit cards and electronic payments have forever changed the way we perceive and use money.

A banking and checking system meant that money was seen less and less frequently in the form of cash. Today, with electronic deposit, automated bill pay, and credit cards, the vast majority of the world's money is nothing more than electronic bytes. Someone making $100,000 this year is likely to see less than $2,000 of that in the form of cash. The rest is out there in cyberspace.

As money has become less constrained, its control has become decentralized. Money now moves more from bottom-up than from top-down. Financial institutions don't have to create currency to create money. They don't need printing presses or armored cars to generate and transport capital all over the globe. When you can buy stock on the Tokyo Exchange or transfer funds to the Bank of Dubai with the click of a mouse, Fort Knox becomes an anachronism. Individuals and institutions are replacing governments as the real controllers of money supply and movement. When a government anywhere in the world gets careless with their monetary policy, world markets can punish them in mere minutes by devaluing their bonds and even their currency through massive sell-offs.

Throughout its history, money has steadily become more abstract over time. Almost frighteningly, money has taken on some of the characteristics of God. Money can now be totally abstract and without corporeal body. Money, like God, requires a certain element of faith in it in order for us to fully benefit. After God, money is the single biggest catalyst for the development of social institutions. While religion creates strong human connections, it also creates strong human divisions. The desire for financial gain is often enough incentive for people of different faiths and cultures to work together. Money can sometimes bring together what religion has torn asunder. Money also enables humans to connect efficiently, if not always effectively.

Over time, money has become the standard value of time. Money first became the standard value for work, and the hourly wage linked the value of work with the value of time. The hourly wage and overtime pay is evidence not only that time is money, but also that more time requires even more money.

While money has not made people think better, it has made them think differently. Money makes it both easier and more tempting for people to think quantitatively, rather than qualitatively.

Money now moves at the speed of light. It can also move at the speed of thought, which makes careful thought more necessary than ever when it comes to decisions about money. Shrinking attention spans and thousands of daily distractions make it hard to give money decisions a proper gestation period. The ability to send your money to anyone anywhere on a whim and a mouse click only compounds the risk of sending your money to a place from whence it ne'er shall return.

Money of today not only has the ability to move from anywhere to anywhere, money of today has an unprecedented ability to be created from the money of tomorrow. Governments can create more money today, but its value today comes in part from its diminished capacity tomorrow, as inflation whittles away its purchasing power in the future. Individuals can transform the money of tomorrow into the money of today with the swipe of a credit card. The problem with moving money from the future to the present is you will then spend the future paying for the past.

Money has never been less restricted than it is today. This freedom of creation and movement of money affords us historic opportunities, but it also creates new and often unseen dangers. Money has never been more essential, while at the same time it has never been more intangible. This modern paradox of money is also the modern paradox of God.

MONEY TIS   MONEY TAIN'T

Carl Jung, the noted Swiss psychiatrist, said, "You are what you do." Forrest Gump, the noted fictional movie character, said, "Stupid is as stupid does." Both expressions sum up the same idea – what someone (or something) *is* will be judged by what that someone or something *does*.

When we look at what money is and isn't, it's helpful to look at what money does. We also need to look at what money doesn't do, as well as what it might do that we shouldn't allow it to do. Remember that money is amoral and inanimate, so whatever money is or does is determined by us, not by it.

As a starting point, we can say that money is anything that's used to make payments and accounting for debts and credits. All Federal Reserve notes (the paper currency printed by the federal government) state that "This note is legal tender for all debts, public and private." Because it's legal tender, paying a debt with U.S. paper currency satisfies the debt (at least in the U.S.), even if the creditor doesn't want to accept payment in that manner. One reason Federal Reserve notes can claim legal tender status is their value is backed by the full faith and credit of the United States government. Also, those Federal Reserve notes can be used to purchase any other form of payment the creditor might prefer, including currencies of other nations.

Money is *fungible*, which doesn't mean it's capable of having fun. If something is fungible, its individual units are capable of mutual substitution. If you deposit ten $100 bills into your bank account and later make a withdrawal of $1,000, you won't receive the same ten $100 bills you deposited. Any $100 bill is interchangeable with any other - that's fungibility.

Currencies of different countries are not fungible, however. Growing up near the Canadian border, I was very aware that Canadian coins did not work in American vending machines. Even if the exchange value of an American dollar and a Canadian dollar are the same (they rarely are), unless both currencies are accepted at all the same places, they're not fungible.

If money is as money does, let's look at some of the functions of money:

- *Unit of account* – Money provides a common unit of account for expressing the market value of widely different goods and services. If something can be valued in money, its value can be compared to anything else that can also be valued in money. If your time can be valued in dollars and an item you want can be valued in dollars, you can calculate how much time you must pay to get the item you want.
  Pitfall – Things that shouldn't be valued in money or have their value compared to other things have it done because money is our default method of assessing value.
- *Store of Value* – Wealth can be held in many forms (stocks, real estate, etc.), but no form of wealth is as readily convertible into other goods or services as is

money. Money can also be accumulated over time, with no upper limits and stored "where moths and rust cannot destroy", though inflation still can.
Pitfall – The ability to store wealth through money can lead to a disconnect between the individual and other people and between the individual and God.

- *Medium of exchange* – Without money, people would have to barter to exchange goods and services. Money eliminates the need for a coincidence of wants. Money facilitates trade because money is generally acceptable to everyone as payment for anything.
  Pitfall – The ability of money to enable the exchange of goods and services can lead to goods and services that shouldn't be valued in money being exchanged for money.
- *Standard of deferred payments* – Because so much of the modern economy is based on credit markets, money is critical for the stability of those markets. Only money can be maintained in such a way that neither debtors nor creditors stand to lose.
  Pitfall – By stabilizing credit markets, money makes credit more tempting and more available, leading to major financial problems for many.

We tend to equate money with currency. Currency is technically money in actual use as a medium of exchange, so while all currency is money, not all money is in the form of currency. When we see a dollar bill, we refer to it as money, not as currency. While that perspective is technically correct, it can be misleading.

Rather than equating money with currency, it's better to equate money with *purchasing power*. Money, currency, and purchasing power may seem synonymous at first, but purchasing power can change drastically, even when the currency is unchanged.

Cost of Living is a rather vague and often misused term. In broad terms, it's a way of measuring changes in purchasing power at different places and at different points in time. The one consistent aspect of the cost of living is that it always seems to be rising.

We know that the cost of living is higher in places like San Francisco than it is in places like Des Moines. Your dollar doesn't go as far in San Francisco as in Des Moines, so if you accept a job transfer from Des Moines to San Francisco, you'll need a substantial raise just to maintain the same standard of living.

Differences in the cost of living between places are easier to comprehend than are differences between points in time. The time differences are also easier to comprehend in hindsight than in foresight. We can see records of home prices in 1960 and recognize that home prices have risen considerably since then. We can also recognize that incomes also rose during that period, so while the number of dollars to buy a home increased over that period of time, the number of hours worked to buy a home may not have, due to increasing incomes.

When we try to think about money in the future, there's a greater tendency to confuse currency with purchasing power. Over time, the nominal value of a dollar is unchanged. One dollar today is still one dollar tomorrow. However, that dollar's market value, what it can purchase, can change drastically over time.

For example, let's say you purchase a 10-year CD at the local bank that will pay 3% compounded annual interest over that ten-year period. At the end of the ten-year period, your $1,000 will have grown to $1,343.92. Not bad.

Unfortunately for you, during that period, inflation averaged 4% per year. With that inflation rate, it would take $1,480.24 to buy in ten years what you could have bought for $1,000 today. In nominal terms, your money increased 34.39%. In purchasing power terms, your money *decreased* 9.08%. Not only did inflation reduce your purchasing power, you never got to enjoy anything that money could have purchased during that ten-year period because it was stuck at the bank, being slowly consumed by inflation. Bummer.

Even if you never took an economics class, you're familiar with the laws of supply and demand. When demand exceeds supply, prices rise until demand and supply even out. When supply exceeds demand, prices fall until equilibrium is reached.

Money is not immune to the laws of supply and demand. When the supply of money grows faster than the supply of goods and services available for purchase, we get *inflation*. The Federal Reserve spends most of its time adjusting the money supply to keep the economy moving while keeping inflation under control.

When the supply of money shrinks, especially if it shrinks faster than the production of goods and services, you get the fairly unusual condition of *deflation*. During the Great Depression there was considerable deflation. The money supply basically froze up, and prices plunged as producers undercut each other on price to get what relatively few dollars were still in circulation.

Circulation is a particularly apt term when we talk about money. Money is like the blood in your body – it's vital for life, yet quite useless if not circulating. Imagine if everyone decided at once they were going to seriously reduce spending and increase saving. The result would be an economic crash, as the lack of spending would reduce everyone's incomes, thus also reducing their ability to save. Such an economic crash, which occurred in 1929 and which we narrowly avoided in 2008, is the financial version of a major heart attack. The parts are still there, but nothing's being pumped, so everything stops.

Saving and spending are both essential to the economy. Spending is what keeps the economy going in the short run. Saving is what keeps it going in the long run. Your personal finances run the same way. Spending may enable a very nice lifestyle in the present, but a lack of savings is sure to create real financial hardships in the future. Going back to our blood circulation analogy, spending is like the circulation of the blood; saving is the blood supply itself. You need both to be healthy.

Benjamin Franklin is credited with saying that time is money, though someone likely made that connection about a day after the first coins were minted in Lydia twenty-five centuries ago. The meaning of that saying is that how you treat your time is also how you treat your money. Time is the one thing everyone has, so it's the one thing everyone can exchange for money. Every day has the same twenty-four hours for everyone on the planet – no other resource is so equally distributed. Wasting that resource is the same as wasting money. How we allocate our time has a greater impact on our financial position than any other single factor.

While time is money to us humans, time is money to money as well. This principle is usually termed *the time value of money*.

We all know that to have any long-term success, including financial security, we need to practice delayed gratification. Delayed gratification is difficult because we live in the present, and our present self is too often willing to seek pleasure at the expense of our future self, as anyone who ever had a hangover can attest. If we're to forego something we want now for something in the future, that something in the future has to be better enough than what we want now to make the wait worthwhile.

That "something" is most typically money, in large part because money can be converted into an almost infinite number of somethings. The temptation in the present is to use your money now to buy something you want (a new car, a vacation, a pair of shoes). To entice you to not buy any of those things now, your money needs to grow over time to enable you to later buy a <u>nicer</u> car, vacation, or pair of shoes (or simply enable you to buy necessities when you no longer earn an income).

Different people need different levels of motivation to delay gratification. Compulsive spenders need a lot of growth in their money to encourage them to save rather than spend. Unfortunately, few legitimate investments offer a sufficient long-term return to dissuade most compulsive spenders from spending. Compulsive savers need little encouragement to delay gratification – they merely spend their time seeking out the best return for their level of risk.

The time value of money is simply an assessment of how much reward is necessary to make it worthwhile to save rather than spend. We learned a moment ago that a 3% return is no incentive to save when inflation is 4%; no one wants to be punished for delaying gratification.

Assessing the time value of money helps in determining how much growth your money needs to have in order to have greater purchasing power in the future. If the money can't buy more of everything in the future, there's no incentive, financial or emotional, to save. In short, a dollar today is worth more than a dollar a year from now, in part because of the loss of purchasing power due to inflation, but also because humans value anything that can be used and enjoyed now more than that same thing at some point in the future.

So far in this chapter our discussion has focused on the aspects of money that are typically discussed in economics textbooks. Knowing that such material can be a little dry, I applaud you for reading to this point. The rest of this chapter will focus on money as a metaphor – discussing what money is and isn't as a representation of something else.

Money Isn't the Cause

You're going to spend some 100,000 hours training for and working at your career(s). You work to get paid, and you work harder hoping to get paid more. So why do I say that money isn't the cause of all that effort?

You aren't working for the money. You're working (hopefully) for two reasons: to give meaning to your life by making a contribution to society by providing your fellow man with needed goods and services. And you're working to provide you and your family with all of the necessities and a few of the luxuries of life. Money has nothing to do with the first reason for working. (If you're getting none of the first reason out of your work, no amount of money can make up for that absence.) As for the second reason, money is a medium of exchange that enables you to efficiently convert your work into those necessities and luxuries that are the actual cause of your work. Never confuse money as the cause of what you do with the real cause of what you do. The real cause is what you use the money for.

If money is acquired through an illegal or immoral process, its use will be tainted by the method of obtainment, regardless of the morality of its use. Money legally acquired that's used for an illegal or immoral purpose is similarly tainted. Both the method of acquiring money and its use must be legal and moral to prevent either being corrupted.

If the cause is the merely the acquisition of money for its own sake, even if it is legally acquired, then the cause is itself bankrupt. The cause of money acquisition must always be something larger than acquisition as its own end. The cause may be providing shelter, saving for old age, helping a destitute stranger, or merely the purchase of an interesting knick-knack. Even a frivolous reason for acquiring money is better than having no reason at all.

Money should never be the end, only the means to an end.

Money Is the Effect

In addition to leading to financial ruin for many families, easy credit has also created a distortion in our understanding of the real cause-and-effect relationship of money. Our ability to acquire almost anything now and pay for it later violates the natural order of the world. Such violations were never possible before the introduction of money and its demented offspring, debt.

Our Cro-Magnon forebears had nothing resembling money, yet they understood the concept of pay-as-you-go. Their environment might have been more accurately described as pay-before-you-go. Their needs were extremely basic: food, clothing, and shelter sufficient to keep them alive through the current season. Two and sometimes all three of these needs could be supplied by what they hunted. But they got nothing until they killed an animal that was highly likely to kill them too in self-defense. There was no deviation from pay-before-you-go, even if it meant starvation. Such an environment was a great catalyst for initiative, teamwork, and thrift.

Fast-forward to the 21st century. Governments, corporations, and individuals in the U.S. have collectively spent to date some four years of future production. In Cro-Magnon terms, settling that debt would require killing four years' worth of meat before you saw your next meal.

Because we've become so accustomed to spending money we haven't yet earned, we've developed a tendency to see money as cause, rather than as effect. It's hard to see money as the effect of our work when the money is spent years before the work to earn it is performed. Money-in-the-present is seen as the motivator to produce more in the future, rather than seeing it in its correct place, as the reward for having produced more in the past. Debt perverts money from effect to cause when money becomes a cause to correct the imbalance in the present created by debt.

On the job, this misplacement of cause and effect creates the misplaced mindset that if my boss would only pay me more, I would be a more productive worker. It never works that way; first, you create higher value; then, you receive higher value. To see money as the cause is akin to standing in front of your fireplace and declaring, "OK, fireplace, give me some heat, and I'll give you some wood." You'll freeze to death while you're waiting.

Money Isn't a Weapon

Let's first clarify what a weapon is. A weapon is a device used to harm another person. If a weapon is used for offensive purposes, its use assumes the desire to harm the other person in some way. Even when a weapon is used for defensive purposes, its effectiveness is based on deterrence backed by the threat of harm. The greater the ability to harm someone, the more effective the weapon. Some items, like a frying pan or money, were not designed to be weapons, but do get used as such on occasion.

With true weapons, it's their use against the other person that creates harm to that person. It would be difficult to argue that discharging money at someone would be harmful. If you gave $1,000 to a heroin addict, it's possible that person may use that money to inject a fatal overdose. But the addict used free will to decide what to do with the money. Money was not the instrument of destruction here.

When people attempt to use money as a weapon, it's usually done by withholding money, not by providing it. A couple going through a bitter divorce may use the withholding of money to extract concessions from the other side. The federal government routinely threatens to withhold funds to compel state and local governments to meet various requirements, from clean air standards to test scores in schools. Going back to the addict analogy, it isn't the supplying of the drug that frightens the addict; it's the withholding of the drug that's frightening.

To be vulnerable to money being used as a weapon against you, you have to have put yourself in a position similar to the addict. You have to need an inflow of money to the extent that any disruption of that inflow is extremely harmful. (We're all vulnerable to some degree.) More important, you have to be dependent on others providing you with your money "fix". I'm not talking about depending on your employer for your paycheck. You earn that paycheck through a fair and voluntary exchange of labor for it. If you lose your job, you can still get another. I'm talking about the person who receives money from others without giving something in return. Whether the money comes from a government program or a domineering parent, they who accept it run the risk of being coerced into behaviors they object to because that seems less repugnant than the loss of funding.

Someone attempting to use money as a weapon runs the risk of unintended consequences. Using money as a weapon is guaranteed to destroy relationships and create enemies. Rarely does someone use money to harm others without harming themselves as well. Money makes a poor weapon, in part because it almost always backfires on its user.

Money Is a Tool

As a former Industrial Arts teacher, I know a little about tools. As a teacher, my first emphasis was always on the proper and safe use of any tool. Lack of proper instruction on safety could lead to misuse of a tool, which typically leads to accidents. Any intentional misuse of a tool would earn you a permanent ban from any and all tools in my shop.

Money that's used to destroy is a weapon, and you know my position on that. Money that's used to build is a tool - the greatest building tool ever devised. To misuse such an incredible tool as a dangerous weapon would warrant a lifetime ban on its future use, if only such a ban could be enforced.

For safety reasons and to avoid lawsuits, tools have all kinds of safety warnings on them. Money, in none of its myriad forms, carries any such safety warning. When determining whether you're using money properly, I recommend referring back to the Golden Rule – would you want to be on the receiving end of someone using money in the same way you're using it? If your answer is no, then you're not using money properly.

There's an old shop teacher saying – when your only tool is a hammer, every problem is a nail. Money's ability to be used now and in the future, to solve enormously varied problems, and to seize equally varied opportunities makes it the best single tool to possess. Money has flexibility of use that puts a Swiss army knife to shame.

And what money is best at building is a future. When used properly, money does not deteriorate over time like most things we build. When properly used and managed, money becomes bigger and better over time, enabling the building of bigger dreams in the future than can be built today. Money creates its own new-and-improved version as it moves forward. It never becomes obsolete. To paraphrase Gershwin: In time the Rockies may crumble / Gibraltar may tumble / they're only made of clay / but money is here to stay.

I used to know some Industrial Arts teachers who were reluctant to use the tools in their shops. They liked to see them all shiny and clean and in their proper place. Letting a bunch of kids use them would mess them up, so they were parsimonious in their use. I could never understand this logic. What else were these tools for? The gain from their use would more than offset the loss from wear and tear. Money should never be a tool that sits unused. It should always be building something – a worry-free retirement, a Ph.D. for a grandchild, protection from catastrophe, whatever is needed and important. It's too great a tool to sit idle.

Money Isn't (a) God

When money is desired only for money's sake, it's the beginning of the worship of money. It's no accident that the Bible mentions money more than any other topic, which is in large part because we're more likely to use money more than anything else in this world as a substitute for the Almighty.

A couple of biblical passages are especially relevant in this conversation. The first is: "The love of money is the root of all evil." Remember, it's the *love* of money, not the money, that's the problem. And the love of money comes from within us, and it's our fault if we allow it to develop. Saying that money is the root of all evil is to try to shift the blame for *our* weakness to an inanimate object. It's like blaming heroin addiction not on the user or the dealer, but on the heroin itself. It's absolving, easy, and wrong.

The other biblical passage of note is: "Render unto Caesar that which is Caesar's, and unto God that which is God's." Our life is spent walking a tightrope between the material world and the spiritual world. Part of awareness involves understanding the relative position of these two worlds and reconciling them to each other. What Jesus is trying to tell us in that passage is to not let the material world dominate the spiritual world, and that money is insignificant in comparison to one's relationship with God.

The amassing of wealth can give us the delusion of self-sufficiency. This delusion makes us believe we don't need other people and that we don't need God. Such pride was considered a sin in times past, weakening the bonds of a society and weakening the bonds between individuals and God. The material world isn't evil; it's merely secondary to the spiritual world. When we allow ourselves to forget that order and make the material world primary, evil actions are an almost inevitable result.

The less the role of God in your life, the more likely you are to ask money to fill that void. This substitution doesn't mean that material wealth and spiritual well-being are mutually exclusive. Many people with a strong spiritual side become very rich, but they do so because they understand money's secondary role in their lives. Those who don't seek to worship a higher being are doomed to worship something of this earth, and money is almost always the default god of choice.

If you need confirmation that money is not a god, look at your money. It says "In God We Trust". It doesn't say "In This We Trust". Even money itself understands its subordinate role in our lives.

Money Is a Legacy

The Nobel Prize has been awarded annually since 1901 for work in the areas of medicine, physics, economics, literature, chemistry, and peace. Among the over 800 recipients are Jimmy Carter, Winston Churchill, Marie Curie, Albert Einstein, Martin Luther King, Jr., Nelson Mandela, Theodore Roosevelt, and Mother Teresa. The Nobel Prize is arguably the most well-known and prestigious award in the world.

Alfred Nobel is known for the prize that bears his name. He funded the Nobel Foundation in the late 1800's with the equivalent of $200 million in today's money. Nobel amassed his great fortune primarily through his invention of dynamite. Wishing to make some kind of atonement for the damage caused by dynamite's use in weapons, he amended his will in 1895 to leave 94% of his fortune to the establishment of the Nobel Prizes. Nobel's dynamite changed our world in positive ways, and it's not his fault that his invention found its way into weaponry. But the world remembers Alfred Nobel, not for the way he earned his money, but for what he did with it.

There are many ways to create a legacy. You can invent (like Nobel), write a book or a song, or lead a people to freedom. Such methods require a skill set very few of us possess. Another way to create a legacy is to give the future something of value through money. And the ability to accumulate money is something almost everyone possesses.

For those who hate the thought of giving up control after their death, money enables a certain measure of control to continue from the grave. Many trusts have been set up that provide ongoing funding, provided certain conditions are met. For example, a grandchild's trust income may be contingent upon completing college. Ideally, any such trust should be structured to maintain certain standards in behavior or performance, but should also be flexible enough to allow changes that enable the money to meet the goal of its donor in changing conditions.

Money's ability to move into the future intact makes it the perfect tool to create a legacy. More than a century after his death, Alfred Nobel's legacy encourages creativity and research, and it rewards people for discoveries and inventions that Nobel could have hardly imagined in the nineteenth century. This ability to touch the future can enable you to fund an education for grandchildren and great-grandchildren you may never meet, but who will know you and love you through your legacy. You can show continued support to causes near and dear to your heart by supporting or even creating a foundation that supports those causes. Your ability to affect the future is limited only by your creativity and your desire to make a difference. Money can't make you immortal, but it can help you get as close to immortality as humans are allowed.

Money Isn't Power

If you read *The Millionaire Next Door*, you get an interesting and surprising portrait of the American millionaire. Millionaires are typically male, have a college degree, are in their mid-50's, own their own business, have been married only once, live well below their means, are actively involved in their community, and are first-generation wealthy. In short, their status as millionaires isn't the result of a love of money; it's the result of extraordinary self-discipline.

It's easy to think that money is power because we often see people with money exerting influence on those without money. We conclude that money is the most obvious difference between the parties, so money must be the reason for the difference in power. What we tend to ignore is the self-discipline and strength of character of the person with money. A person with such traits is able to exert enormous influence over people without the introduction of personal wealth. History is full of such people: Martin Luther King, Jr., Gandhi, Abraham Lincoln, Joan of Arc, Jesus.

Exerting influence is not the same as exerting power. Influence involves persuasion and leading people in a direction they want to move, but may not have the knowledge or courage to do so. Power involves using negative reinforcement to compel someone to do something they wouldn't do without the threat of harm - physical, financial, or otherwise. You use influence on your friends; you use power against your enemies.

People who've accumulated money through hard work, self-discipline and honesty have few enemies. When we see someone using money to compel others to act against their own self-interest, it's likely the person with money didn't obtain it with integrity. If their money had been acquired through hard work, self-discipline and honesty, they'd have more respect for that money and would use it more carefully. People who misuse money in such a manner eventually have it taken away from them. Their character flaws make it almost impossible to control such a valuable asset for a long time. Their ability to control money is undermined by their inability to control themselves.

Many wealthy people equate their money with power; this equation is a primary reason they wanted to acquire wealth. Such people are weak, and they equate money with power because they equate a lack of money with weakness. Children bully with words and fists; adults bully with money. The ability to be bullied by people with money is first and foremost the result of an inability to rule money in one's own life. Someone with an understanding of money and self-discipline about money is immune from anyone attempting to use money to get them to act against their own self-interest.

Money is power against you only if you are under the power of money.

Money Is Dignity and Freedom

It's no secret that status is highly correlated with money. The list of wealthiest people and the list of highest incomes in America are studied each year with great interest. They're the American version of a register of royalty. But the status that money may create isn't the same as dignity.

Status is something that's conveyed by other people to an individual. Dignity is something that individuals convey to themselves. Dignity is a measure of your self-respect. It must be earned for yourself, and it can't be taken away by others.

Few things generate self-respect like a dollar earned through honest labor. When humans, especially the young, don't sacrifice for the money they get, they respect the money and themselves less. Self-esteem, like money, must be earned to be appreciated.

The ability to accumulate money out of earnings is a great source of dignity. People who save regularly show discipline and foresight. The increasing value of their savings is a double source of pride – they've earned the money *and* they haven't spent the money. People with little savings, especially if they make a good income, are reminded by their low savings balance that they've failed to exercise self-discipline. In the end, true self-respect is the product of self-discipline.

Earning money is also the world's way of saying your work is valued. The world at large can be a cold, calculating place. The only consistent way a complex environment like the modern world can tell people thank you for their efforts is to give them money. A paycheck is the world's most popular thank-you note.

It's important not to place too much emphasis on the size of the paycheck when it comes to assessing your self-worth. Several hedge fund managers have "earned" over a billion dollars annually. What compensates one fund manager could compensate 20,000 teachers. No one, not even a hedge fund manager, is stupid enough to think that those compensation figures accurately reflect the relative contributions of these two jobs to society. Any one of those 20,000 teachers has earned as much dignity as the hedge fund manager, even if they didn't earn as much money.

Recent surveys of doctors showed more than half of them would like to quit the medical profession, mostly because of the aggravation of dealing with insurance companies and other bureaucrats. Almost none of them do quit because almost none of them could match the income they make as doctors in any other field, and because they're spending all of their income now. They're shackled to their current job by its high income.

Money spent can create a prison, but money saved can create freedom. The smaller your financial liabilities and the larger your financial assets, the greater is your freedom. One of the advantages of living well below your means is that jobs that pay less than you currently make are a viable alternative because you can make that change without hurting your standard of living. Those unhappy doctors have limited their options inasmuch as they haven't limited their spending.

Money that generates an income can free you of the burden of generating an income. Money's ability to make money is greater than yours. The day may come when you don't want to work. The day will almost certainly come when you can't work. Money can give you the freedom to stop working when the time comes. Just as important, money enables you to have the dignity of leaving on your own terms.

Money Isn't Character

"Just because you are a character doesn't mean that you have character." opines Winston Wolfe in *Pulp Fiction*. To extend Mr. Wolfe's line of thought further, just because you have money doesn't mean you have character. Character in this sense refers to moral or ethical strength, integrity, fortitude.

In America we admire wealth to such a degree that we often assume the people who have wealth are admirable as well. At the same time, there can be a certain envy of the wealthy, which can make us think less of them because of their wealth. What's your reaction to the name *Donald Trump*? For most people, there's a definite reaction, either positive or negative. A Donald Trump is either admired as a person for his financial success or reviled because he seems to rub everyone's nose in it. What's your reaction to the name *Warren Buffett*? I'm guessing it's a more muted reaction. Although Warren Buffett's net worth is at least fifteen times Donald Trump's, Buffett doesn't elicit many negative reactions. This juxtaposition is due in large part to people's perceptions that Warren Buffett doesn't seek the spotlight and doesn't seem to be purposely reminding us of his wealth and success.

In truth, most people of wealth are also people of good character. Since most wealthy people in this country made it through hard work and sacrifice (Buffett and Trump included), it's safe to assume their character is an asset to them and a large reason for their financial success. Very few of the wealthy are known by the general public. I recognize only a few names on the Forbes 400 list of richest Americans. You probably know a millionaire or three. There's a good chance you don't know they're wealthy, though. Most people who accumulate wealth are discreet about their wealth. The guy you know who flaunts his "wealth" is likely a couple of missed paychecks away from bankruptcy. When you've got it, you don't need to flaunt it.

A person of good character possesses the traits that make them immune to the negative aspects of money. A person possessing loyalty, integrity, discipline, honesty and generosity instinctively knows the limitations of money. A person of good character doesn't expect money to provide human qualities that can only be generated from within. If you're a person of good character, you can't be bought, and you would never "sell out" someone else or yourself.

Money isn't character, but it can reveal character. How someone earns money and how he spends it reveals his priorities, and priorities reveal character. Someone of good character will earn money honestly, save it seriously, spend it carefully, and give it generously. Man makes the money; money doesn't make the man (or woman).

Money Is a Mirror

My mother was orphaned as an infant. She bounced around different foster homes until her early teens, when she was taken in by Mil and Ed Prevost. Mil was a teacher, and Ed was a security guard at a GM plant; they also had an eight-year-old son when my mother went to live with them. They raised her as their own until she married my father at age twenty-two. Mil and Ed took in my mother when she was immersed in those difficult teenage years, which were likely made even more difficult by the traumas my mother had endured to that time.

That selfless act alone tells you a lot about Mil and Ed. I learned something else several years ago that gives another glimpse into their souls. One year they got a notice from the IRS that they were being audited. The reason – the amounts they were claiming for charitable deductions were way out of line with the IRS guidelines for normal legitimate claims. They would have to report to the IRS office and show proof that their deductions were legitimate.

Since Mil and Ed were as honest and meticulous as they were charitable, it was no problem for them to produce the necessary documentation. Keep in mind, to draw the scrutiny of the IRS in such a matter, your claimed deductions would have to be well above 10% of your income. They probably gave that much to their church alone, as they were the type to take the obligation to tithe seriously. For two people who gave some of their best years to a girl who was previously a stranger, giving a substantial part of their income to charity was an easy, natural thing to do.

Many people contend that how we allocate our time reflects our priorities, and our character. While I don't disagree with that contention, I contend that how we allocate our money offers an even more accurate reflection. While both time and money are valuable resources, our money balance is known, while our time balance is not. This difference makes a unit of time less valuable than a unit of money, as we're less aware of its finiteness.

If you analyzed how you allocated your money over the last year, what would it reveal about you? A sizable portion probably went to necessities. By necessities, I mean food, clothing, shelter, transportation, and medical. Within those categories, not every dollar spent is a necessity. The mortgage money on a $200,000 house is likely all necessity. The mortgage money on a $500,000 house is unlikely all necessity. If you like to shop at Neiman-Marcus and the Mercedes dealership, very little of those expenses qualify as necessities.

How much did you spend on luxuries? How much did you set aside for future obligations, including obligations to yourself? How much went to help family members? How much went to help those less fortunate than you? How much did you spend that was borrowed from the future? You may not have much control over the size of your income, but you do have control over how you allocate it.

Money is a mirror; it isn't a photograph. Others know your image from photos, not from a reflection. But photos can be altered; reflections cannot. You see your reflection in the mirror and it shows you as you are. The way you use money reflects your heart and soul in the same way.

Money Isn't Happiness

If you ever doubt the uniqueness or greatness of the United States, remember these words, *the pursuit of happiness*. No other nation in the history of the world has ever embedded an individual's pursuit of happiness as an inalienable right.

Dale Carnegie said, "Success is getting what you want; happiness is wanting what you get." Dr. Albert Schweitzer said, "Success isn't the key to happiness;

happiness is the key to success." It's easy to assume that with success comes happiness. For success to also bring happiness, the goal one is seeking must be correctly perceived. One of the worst feelings a person can experience is, after achieving success with great effort, they end up thinking, "This isn't what I thought it would be."

Just as it's important not to equate success with happiness, it's also important not to confuse happiness with pleasure. Pleasure usually involves an external stimulus, is mostly physical in nature, and is short-lived. Happiness involves thoughts and emotions and is generated internally, not externally. The act of procreation (generally) gives pleasure. Holding your newborn child in your arms brings happiness.

Money can buy pleasure, but not happiness, in the same way that money can buy books, but not wisdom. Pleasure involves receiving. Happiness involves giving. It's not only more blessed to give than receive, it also brings greater happiness. In one research study, people were given $100. The first group was instructed to spend it on themselves; the second group was instructed to spend it on others or to give it away. The second group reported happiness measures resulting from their actions that were *four times higher* than the first group.

Money can bring pleasure in its accumulation, but it can bring happiness only through its distribution. I don't mean distribution to a car payment, medical bill, or tax liability. I mean distribution to someone or something that benefits others, and not you, and that is made voluntarily. I mean charity.

Several studies over several decades have confirmed certain correlations between money and happiness. First, it's harder to be happy when you're poor. Your ability to give is hampered, and you're focused on survival. Once basic needs are met, more money barely moves the happiness meter. Buying more stuff brings short-lived pleasure, then disappointment. The disappointment of no happiness is compounded by the disappointment of less money. Finally, avarice, an extreme desire for wealth, is a cause of great unhappiness. The pursuit of money for money's sake becomes all-consuming and gives nothing in return.

Happiness comes from the inside out, and money can create happiness only if it moves the same way. Happiness for yourself is the product of creating happiness for others. It's a never-ending upward spiral.

Money Is Hope

"Hope is a good thing; maybe the best of things. And no good thing ever dies." So writes Andy Dufresne in *The Shawshank Redemption*, one of the best movies about hope ever made. Andy's friend Red, who is finally released after forty years of hopeless incarceration, ends the movie with the words, "I hope." Hope is the fuel of all progress, of all success, and of all happiness. It's impossible to be optimistic without hope in your heart.

In addition to freedom, the other ingredient that turned Andy and Red's hopes into reality was money. Without money, the happy ending wouldn't have happened. Without money, many of our hopes for the future get compromised or crushed altogether. In addition to hard work, sacrifice, determination, and optimism, many dreams require money to motivate the outside world to assist in making those dreams a reality.

One of the most fundamental of human hopes is that your children will enjoy greater opportunity than you had. One of the best ways to increase your child's opportunities is to make sure they get a good education. At the very least, that means a four-year college degree with a $25,000 price tag for tuition alone. Without the ability to pay for it, hopes for a college degree and the opportunities the degree will afford may soon be crushed. Paying for college is just the most common example of how money affects the hopes we have for our children.

Money also affects our hopes for our own future. We hope our investments will do what they're supposed to do so we can retire as planned. We hope that raise comes through so we can get a new car. We hope we don't get laid off and have to sell our house. We hope our parents don't have to go to a nursing home because we'll have to pay for it, dashing our hopes for a lot of our future plans.

The one type of hope that is counterproductive is hoping for a longshot. When it comes to money, such false hope includes any kind of gambling, but especially long chance games like the lottery. The money spent on such activities is no longer available for more productive uses, and hoping for such a payoff is likely to keep you from devoting time and money to those activities that can actually pay off. Money is hope, which is very different than hoping for money.

Hope is the ultimate motivator. Hope enables us to work hard, delay gratification, set priorities, and remain disciplined. Money can help us realize our hopes, but it's hope itself that motivates us to act in ways that enable us to accumulate wealth.

Money Isn't Human

With the creation of money, we also created the ability to quantify almost every aspect of life. Money grew beyond its traditional roles as a store of value, a medium of exchange, and a unit of account to become the measuring stick for almost every activity in our lives. Unfortunately, using money as a measurement has also led to money being used as a replacement for human activities, interactions, emotions, and affections.

Money is easily the most powerful secular force in the world. I can think of only four motivators to Americans that might be stronger than money – they are God, family, country, and sex. For the great majority of Americans, at least one of these four trumps money in importance. But that still leaves money as a powerful influence on a large number of people, here and around the world.

Even for these four strong motivators, money is a factor. We may prefer to give God our treasure instead of our time or our talent because it's easier. Much, often too much, of the family dynamic revolves around money. We love our country, but that doesn't stop us from complaining about and possibly fudging on our taxes. And money-for-sex isn't the world's oldest profession by accident.

Money is our main method of contact with the outside world. Money enables us to have greater contact with the outside world, although it's largely on a superficial transaction basis. When money starts being used as a substitute in our closest relationships, we risk becoming less human.

We don't give of ourselves if it's easier to give money. We don't owe gratitude; we just owe money.

Money greatly enabled and simplified transactions, but a consequence is we tend to think of relationships as transactions. Mutually beneficial relationships are based on reciprocity, but reciprocity can be difficult to measure, and the people in the relationship may have vastly differing perceptions of the equality of the reciprocity. The natural inclination is to revert to money to settle any disputes of inequality.

When we use money to substitute for the giving of ourselves, we devalue that which wasn't given. By putting a dollar figure on that which each of us can uniquely offer from our hearts, we take something that was priceless and make it almost worthless.

The worst use of money is when we attempt to measure our humanity with money. Faith, love, kindness, and loyalty can't be measured by money, or at least not by money alone. To use money in such a manner debases the giver and insults the receiver. Money can be used to enhance our humanity, enabling us to reach out to more people. It should never be used to enable us to reach out less.

Money Is Love

Let me make very clear what I mean by the above statement. Money is excellent as an *expression* of love. It is horrible as a *substitute* for love.

Because money is so flexible in its use, it can express love in ways that are impossible otherwise. A loved one may have a disease you can't even pronounce, much less treat. But if treatment exists, money can obtain it. You don't have to be a college graduate to enable your grandchild to become one. You don't have to know anything about computers to provide start-up funding for your entrepreneurial geek son to create the next Google.

With money, you don't have to *know* a lot to help; you only have to *care* a lot to help.

Money, as an expression of love, has no time frame. You can express love to those who have passed away by establishing a memorial fund to help a cause they supported. You can express love in the present by the simple act of buying a gift for someone for no special reason. You can express love in the future by sending money into the future to help those who will live in that future, even if you aren't one of them.

Money, as an expression of love, is definitely more emotional than logical, because love is that way, too. That imbalance doesn't mean that logic and discipline should be thrown out the window when it comes to intersecting money and love. You may love a son or daughter, but if they have a drug problem, giving them money that makes the problem worse isn't love. Expressing love with money means that giving or withholding money is done to help the other person, never to hurt them. Your loved one may not share your perspective, but you're more likely to have the correct perspective in such cases. Feelings of doubt or guilt should not accompany any giving of money as an expression of love.

One other thing – you can't love money. Love is humanity's greatest gift from God. Money is mentioned more times than love in the Bible, but love is clearly the most important thing, from the Ten Commandments to the Gospels. Love is intended for that which can recognize love. Money can express love – it can't recognize it or reciprocate it.

THE HUMANNESS OF HUMANITY

At some point in your life, you've probably read about or heard a sermon on the *Seven Deadly Sins*. The modern concept of the seven deadly sins is linked to a 4th century monk, Evagrius Ponticus. In AD 590, Pope Gregory I revised the list, and when Dante included the seven deadly sins in *The Divine Comedy* around 1300, their recognition became widespread. To refresh your memory, the seven deadly sins are:

- Lust – an intense desire, typically sexual
- Gluttony – overindulgence (also selfishness)
- Greed – includes avarice
- Sloth – failure to do one's duty
- Wrath – uncontrolled anger or rage
- Envy – insatiable desire for what isn't yours
- Pride – self-love that leads to the other deadly sins

The seven deadly sins are considered the sins to which we're most susceptible, due to our human nature, our *humanness*, if you will. The Catholic Church, which considers these seven sins serious enough offenses to God that they merit the term "deadly", also compiled a list of *Seven Heavenly Virtues*, practices that would prevent the introduction of those sins into one's life. The seven virtues and their corresponding sins are:

- Chastity (Lust)
- Temperance (Gluttony)
- Charity (Greed)
- Diligence (Sloth)
- Patience (Wrath)
- Kindness (Envy)
- Humility (Pride)

Life would be a lot less complicated if we could simply avoid the seven deadly sins by practicing the seven virtues. Yet, to paraphrase Lincoln, some of us can do it some of the time, but none of us can do it all of the time. One reason none of us can avoid all of these sins all of the time is our physical body and tens of thousands of years of genetic tinkering that created the human race as we know it today.

The first thing to recognize about humans is that our brains have been roughly the same for roughly the last 200,000 years. We've essentially maxed out on brain size because if our heads get any bigger, childbirth will become extremely dangerous, if not impossible. We don't need more capacity, though. It's our programming that's badly in need of updating.

Human beings aren't neurologically well-designed to live in abundance. Our brains evolved over thousands of years in an environment of scarcity. Our natural reward pathways instruct us to get all we can while we can because tomorrow there's likely to be nothing. This instinct, which at the very least triggers lust, gluttony, and greed, is also the instinct most responsible for the human race surviving against all odds to become the planet's dominant species.

An excellent example of how we're hardwired to deal with scarcity is dieting. Most people, when they go on a diet, do it the wrong way. Instead of modestly decreasing calorie intake and modestly increasing calorie output through exercise, the typical diet involves a drastic change in eating patterns which includes a sudden and substantial reduction in calorie intake.

The body doesn't like such sudden changes. It interprets a sudden and substantial decrease in calories not as mere scarcity, but as famine. It goes into famine mode by requiring as few calories as possible to maintain the body and perform physical tasks. This adjustment is one reason why weight loss slows down rapidly after the first few days or weeks.

To make matters worse, any extra calories the body receives are immediately assigned to fat, as insurance against the next famine. This reallocation of calories is the reason most people end up gaining more weight than they lost once they go off their diet. The body's first job is survival, and its instruction manual was written many millennia ago when lust, gluttony, and greed were more like virtues than vices.

Sloth is synonymous with laziness, though sloth may be more accurately defined as not doing something to some minimum standard, which is pretty much assured if one is lazy. Even laziness has a valid role in our collective history.

Our early ancestors survived by hunting. One of the most common forms of hunting was *persistence hunting*, where several people would cull an animal from a herd and literally run it to death. Our ancestors could do this because we evolved to run longer without overheating than any of the prey of the time. The problem with persistence hunting was that no one knew at the start of the hunt if they'd be running five miles or twenty that day, so when there was an opportunity to do nothing, that was the best thing to do.

We aren't exactly hardwired to do nothing, but we are hardwired to expend as little energy as possible in getting something done. We're always looking, consciously or unconsciously, for shortcuts. Just as only the most efficient businesses survive, the same holds true for individuals in a species and for entire species.

One way we minimize our energy use is through the development of habits. Typically, habits develop without conscious effort. In fact, the whole concept of habit is that habits minimize conscious effort. When something becomes a habit (making breakfast, driving to work, etc.), we expend physical effort but very little thought to getting the task done. Habits let us perform tasks on auto-pilot, saving our brain's energy usage for other tasks. And because the brain is an energy glutton, consuming 20% of our calories, anything that reduced the demand for energy improved chances for survival in the prehistoric world.

It's hard to make a case for envy as a positive force back then, except as a motivator to wage war on other peoples. Such actions might benefit one's tribe, but not the human race as a whole. Even wrath and pride served a purpose for our ancestors. And while they may not have had a name for it in ancient times, our ancestors, like us, were guilty of *schadenfreude*, that child of envy which is our joy at the misfortunes of those whose position is better than ours.

Wrath, or the threat of incurring it, kept members of the tribe in line. To be ostracized from one's tribe was a death sentence back then. The only way humans ever survived in the wilderness was by placing the needs of the group above the desires of the individual, though such behavior often had to be enforced. When an individual became too selfish, they threatened the survival of the group and had to be dealt with.

Pride served a purpose in bringing leaders to the fore. Pride is self-love that can lead to the other deadly sins, but throughout history, humble leaders have been few and far between. Humans, then as now, gravitate to the person who inspires confidence that they can lead the people to where they need to go.

The fact that most of the seven deadly sins may have served a purpose in prehistoric times doesn't mean we get a pass on committing them today. It does at least help to know that the *desire* to commit these sins has to do with the way we evolved, not through some personal failing. Nevertheless, we're each responsible for our actions stemming from our desires. Blaming the devil or your DNA isn't likely to get you a reprieve from judgment.

Few of God's creatures have proven as adaptable as humans. Our ability to adapt to our environment enabled us to migrate to all parts of the planet, which prevented our extinction on more than one occasion in history. Our lifespan is a nonstop series of adaptations as we progress from infancy to old age, during which time we adapt to changes in marital status, parenthood, employment, residence, and too many others to mention.

Adaptation has its downside as well. Just as we're able to adapt to conditions beyond our control, including changes for the worse, we also adapt to improvements in our condition. A desire fulfilled quickly becomes a necessity.

If you made a list of things we consider necessities today (air conditioning, automobiles, college degrees, internet, antibiotics, TV, and thousands more), the list would be a very long one. You might then pause to realize that, because of these thousands of inventions, most Americans have a better overall quality of life than did the Rockefellers, Vanderbilts, and Carnegies of the Gilded Age at the end of the 19th century.

In fact, it's been estimated that the average American today has a higher standard of living than 99.9% of the entire human population throughout history. For many of us, the only time we realize how much we've adapted to our high standard of living is when we go to a place where the standard of living is much lower. Such travels give us a renewed appreciation for our blessings, but, because we're so good at adapting, that appreciation diminishes as we re-adapt to life back home.

Our ability to adapt quickly to improvements can make it hard to consistently feel gratitude. Any privilege that lasts more than a day becomes an entitlement. Quickly adapting to improvements may be a spur to "progress", but it also impedes our ability to appreciate all we have now.

Joni Mitchell sang about not knowing what we've got til it's gone. We often don't fully appreciate something (or someone) until we suffer a loss.

People don't like losing, and I'm not just referring here to games. *Loss aversion* is a well-documented trait, though it's not unique to our species. Animals, including humans, fight harder to prevent losses than to achieve gains. Defenders succeed more than aggressors, which is why winning a war of aggression is so hard, even when the aggressor has superior power. All animals instinctively know to focus more on avoiding danger than on seizing opportunities – survival depends more on the former than the latter.

Loss aversion, as we use it here, means that our response to losses is stronger than our response to corresponding gains. Studies have shown the difference in that ratio is about two to one. In other words, the bad feeling you get from losing $100 is twice as strong as the good feeling you get from gaining $100.

For financial outcomes, the usual reference point is the status quo, though it can often be an expected outcome or an outcome to which we feel entitled. Outcomes that are better than the reference point are interpreted as gains; those that are worse are interpreted as losses. For example, a 5% raise would be felt as a gain if you weren't expecting any raise. However, if you were expecting and/or felt entitled to a 10% raise, the 5% raise could end up feeling like a loss.

We're risk averse when it comes to gains, but risk seeking when it comes to losses. People tend to become more conservative as they become wealthier because they have more to lose. The tendency of the wealthy to be politically conservative isn't politics; it's economics, with some psychology, too.

Loss aversion is a powerful force. It favors minimal changes in the status quo because change creates uncertainty and the possibility of loss. Those who have little to lose and those who've already lost understandably have less aversion to losses. They don't mind changing the status quo.

When faced with the high probability of a large loss, we not only aren't risk averse, we become risk seekers. The losing side in a war continues fighting long after defeat becomes inevitable. Gamblers on a losing streak behave the same way.

Here's a simple experiment that's been done countless times in college classrooms. You're given

$1,000. You can now accept or decline a bet on a coin flip – if you win, you'll get another $1,000; if you lose, you'll have to give back the $1,000. Which do you choose? By about three to one, most people decline the bet and keep the money.

In the second part of the experiment, you must give up $1,000 of your own money. You can now accept or decline a bet on a coin flip – if you win, you'll get your $1,000 back; if you lose, you'll have to give up an additional $1,000. Which do you choose? The same people in these experiments, when faced with this choice, by the same three to one margin accept the bet.

Both bets are identical in terms of the amount at stake and the probability of winning or losing. The only difference is the reference point. In the first part of the experiment, the subjects experience a financial gain and don't want to give it up, so they become averse to the risk of loss. In the second part, the subjects experience a financial loss and seek a way to eliminate the loss, which requires them to accept risks they wouldn't usually accept.

It may seem incongruous, but the poor are often more risk averse than the rich. The poor (and misers) tend to interpret all costs as losses. Their funds are too dear to part with, so even a prudent expenditure can feel like a loss. It's one reason why brand names sell better in poor neighborhoods than store brands. When your funds are limited, you can't risk that the store brand won't be of acceptable quality, so you pay the extra for the name brand as insurance against such a loss.

Humans are either subject to, or creators of, an amazing number of biases. Let's look at a few that can affect us financially.

Hindsight is 20/20, which is a familiar way of saying we suffer from *hindsight bias*. Hindsight bias might also be called the I-knew-it-all-along effect. When events surprise us, we revise our view of the event to explain how the event could've happened. We don't like to think we could've been blindsided by something unexpected, so we reprogram our memory to look less obtuse. After 9/11, one journalist opined that the main reason the event so shocked us was we suffered from a lack of imagination when it came to terrorism. (In fairness, who could've imagined such monstrosity before it happened?) A Swedish proverb says it best: The afternoon knows what the morning never suspected.

The worse the consequence, the greater the hindsight bias will be. And hindsight bias is especially unkind to agents for others, like physicians, politicians, and financial advisors. We tend to blame these agents for good decisions that had a bad outcome and give them too little credit for successes because they seem obvious in hindsight. We forget that the "handwriting on the wall" is written in invisible ink that only becomes visible later.

The illusion that we understand the past, the result of hindsight bias, feeds the illusion that we can predict and control the future. In truth, we were far worse at knowing what was going to happen and are far worse at knowing what will happen than we think we are. Even so, we look for people, like economists, who can tell us what our financial future will look like. We do this even though research has discovered the economists' predictions are wrong more than half the time. A coin toss would give you a better glimpse into the future.

Unless you're very unhappy, you're probably quite cautious when it comes to change. This aversion to change has a definite connection to our aversion to loss – we worry that change will make things worse, that we'll lose something we currently have.

These feelings are expressed in such phrases as "Better the devil you know." and "We've always done it this way." What's actually being expressed is known as *status quo bias*. The status quo is the default condition, and it takes a convincing argument to get people to make a change, even when they express dissatisfaction with the status quo. The approval rating of Congress is around 15%, yet 85% of the incumbents seeking re-election will win. Such inconsistencies reflect status quo bias.

You might think that the status quo has a better chance of being overturned when the number of alternatives increases. In reality, the opposite is true. When we're faced with an overwhelming number of choices (more than seven qualifies in most cases), the status quo, if there is one, becomes the default choice. The more choices we have, the more research we have to do to determine which the best alternative is. And since we hate to make a change if that change makes things worse, the best thing to do is nothing. The status quo – it's the devil you know.

Status quo bias isn't limited to sticking with the same investments or breakfast cereal. We're also averse to change when it comes to our spiritual lives. New doctrines, and even new perspectives on current doctrines, are greeted warily and even hostilely at times. Think about your particular worship service. I know at my church, if we change a hymn or rearrange the order of events in the service, there will be a group strongly opposed. They don't oppose the change because it's worse; they don't even know if it'll be worse. They oppose it simply because it's *different*. Without realizing it, we often prefer the devil we know to the angels we don't.

We feel a connection with the status quo that we don't feel with any of the alternatives. In a sense, we own the status quo, which is one reason we rate it more highly than the alternatives. We tend to rate what we own higher than anything else, and certainly higher than anyone else would rate what is ours. This overrating of what is ours is known as the *endowment effect*.

Realtors deal with the endowment effect on a daily basis. Realtors know what the market says a house is worth, but that figure rarely rises to what the owner/seller of the house thinks it's worth. We think our house is worth more than it is because of the endowment effect. It isn't just a house – it's our <u>home</u>, and our home is perhaps our most prized possession.

The term pride of ownership can refer to caring for what is yours, but also to overvaluing what is yours. The endowment effect can be easily measured by the difference between what the market is willing to pay for something and the price the seller is willing to accept. The stronger the endowment effect, the bigger the gap.

The endowment effect doesn't just apply to objects. If you've spent any time on Facebook, you've doubtless spent too much time looking at pictures of other people's children, pets, meals, and countless other objects of affection. The people who post these pictures find their subjects of far greater interest and value than do the people who view them. That's only natural – you should find <u>your</u> children and pets of greater value than anyone else's. It's a good idea, though, to remember the endowment effect when posting – no one finds your life as fascinating as you do.

We don't determine value in a vacuum – we determine value in large part by making comparisons. When we make a financial decision, we try to use reference points. What we use in comparison can have a large effect on the value we ultimately determine for something. Determining the value of something by comparing it to others is known as *anchoring*.

What someone uses as an anchor can determine whether a purchase seems like a bargain or a ripoff. For example, a husband might have a desire for a Corvette. In making his case to his wife, he would use as his anchor very expensive cars like Ferrari and Porsche. He would argue that the Corvette is comparable to these cars at a fraction of the price.

The wife would use a different anchor. She might look at a Toyota or a Honda and argue that those cars can provide a similar level of safe, reliable transportation at a fraction of the cost of the Corvette. In his eyes, the Corvette is a bargain; in hers, it's a ripoff.

The example above illustrates the behavior of anchoring and an associated behavior known as *framing*. The husband used a more expensive car as an anchor and framed his presentation to make his choice look like a bargain. By choosing a contrasting anchor, the wife totally reframed the proposition.

We use anchors and framing in our spiritual lives, too. The tithe in Judeo-Christian teachings and the zakat in Islam are anchors to help people determine how much they should give to others. A popular topic on Hindu blog sites deals with dana or charity. The lack of anchors for dana in Hinduism actually creates no small amount of consternation about how much to give. People like anchors as guidelines as long as they're guidelines and not rigid requirements.

Framing is very important when it comes to intangible subjects like the afterlife. In my opinion, the threat of Hell is too often used to promote proper behavior here on earth. I believe a more effective method of behavior modification is to extol the benefits of Heaven. Sometimes framing is nothing more than replacing a stick with a carrot (or vice versa).

"In for a penny, in for a pound" is an old English saying that has more than one meaning. It originally referred to the fact that if one owed a penny (pence), they might as well owe a pound, as the penalties for non-payment of either were about the same. The more common interpretation is that, once having started something, you must see it through to its conclusion, regardless of cost. Such an interpretation merits the reminder that what is perseverance in a good cause is obstinacy in a bad one.

Obstinacy is usually the result when someone succumbs to the *sunk cost fallacy.* In business, a sunk cost is any cost that has already been incurred and that can't be recovered. Sunk costs should have no impact on future plans.

For example, a company may have just spent a million dollars upgrading their computer systems. New improvements since then create a situation where, if the company spends another million dollars to upgrade their computers again, they can save two million dollars. This may seem like a no-brainer, but the idea that a million dollar expenditure has suddenly become obsolete can cause managers to resist the idea of spending more.

Individuals fall victim to sunk cost fallacy even more than businesses. If you've ever held on to an investment that lost value, waiting for it to get back to its purchase price before you sell, you've been a victim of sunk cost fallacy. In almost all such cases, you would've been far better off to sell the investment at a loss and move the proceeds into a more productive asset.

The sunk cost fallacy isn't always bad, though. If your place of worship is going through crisis and change, the best thing may be to say you've got a lot invested there, too much to just give up and walk away.

There are three different criteria for assessing if an object or experience is looked on unfavorably or favorably: *expectations*, *experience*, and *remembrance*.

There's a saying that the two happiest days in a boat owner's life are the day he buys it and the day he sells it. In such cases, it's safe to say that expectations far exceeded the experience. A big part of my job as a financial planner is managing people's expectations about their money and what it can do for them. The more realistic your expectations are, the lower your chances for disappointment.

For the boat owner, the experience of being in the boat, enjoying the sun, skimming across the surface of a pristine lake probably met his expectations. But the experience also included hauling the boat to and from the lake, dealing with lots of other boats and their owners, maintenance, repair, towing, and storage expenses, and no room in the garage because the boat lives there now. Our expectations of our experience rarely include the negative experiences, or at least we don't give them their proper weight.

When it comes to our final evaluation of an object or an experience, it's remembrance that rules the day. Our remembrance is formed at two points – how we felt at the peak (good or bad) and how we felt at the end. How we feel at the end also affects how we evaluate the peak. Experiments with pain have shown that people who receive higher pain that tapers off at the end view the experience as less painful than lower maximum pain levels that continue right to the end. Performers know these facts instinctively. They know to save the best for last and to "always leave 'em wanting more".

Remembrances are affected by the "gauze of memory". As time passes, we tend to remember the positive aspects of an experience and repress the more negative ones. As an example, people, especially older people, have fonder memories of high school than their actual experiences would warrant. Some of that discrepancy can be explained by an appreciation for youth and its possibilities that only comes with age. While fond memories can be a comfort in old age, we have to be careful that distorted memories don't compromise the promise of the future or minimize our appreciation of the present. The good ol' days may have been good, but probably not as good as we remember.

"Viewers don't want to *be* informed. Viewers want to *feel* informed." Those are the words of Chet Collier, one of the founders of Fox News. Please take a moment to ponder the potential impact of Mr. Collier's statement.

People might be insulted or even outraged that someone responsible for one of the largest news organizations in the U.S. thinks that we prefer the illusion of truth than the truth itself. But Mr. Collier knows something about his viewers that they don't know about themselves.

There's a reason why Americans are more polarized than ever. Some may argue that media on the right and left are polarizing forces, while some may argue that they're merely exploiting the polarization. In truth, Americans are becoming more polarized because it's what we *want*. And we want it because it's easier.

Feeling informed is easy; being informed takes work. I'm not talking about the work of studying the issues and seeking the truth. Everyone thinks they do that. The work I'm talking about involves seeking out information and opinions that may well clash with what you know and how you think about certain topics. I'm talking about challenging your own precepts.

People seek consistency in their perceptions and beliefs. What happens when one of our beliefs conflicts with another previously held belief? The term *cognitive dissonance* is used to describe the discomfort that results from holding two conflicting beliefs. Cognitive dissonance can also result when one's actions conflict with one's beliefs.

Cognitive dissonance has only been recognized since the 1950s, but perhaps the best known example of it is over 2,500 years old – Aesop's *The Fox and the Grapes*. In the fable, the fox badly wants some grapes that turn out to be just out of reach. To mollify himself, the fox decides the grapes were sour and not worth having.

Consciously or unconsciously, humans try to avoid cognitive dissonance. When avoidance isn't possible, we engage in dissonance reduction in one of four ways:

1. Change behavior/cognition (Stop doing the thing that creates the conflict.)
2. Justify behavior/cognition by changing the conflicting cognition (It's OK to cheat once in a while.)
3. Justify/behavior cognition by adding new cognitions (Perform some act to offset the offensive act.)
4. Ignore/deny any information that conflicts with existing beliefs.

This last entry is the cause of our increasing polarization. Now that we have media sources that cater to various positions, we actually get support for ignoring or denying alternate views on a subject. Recognizing only information that reinforces our beliefs is known as *confirmation bias*. We're biased in favor of any information that supports our point of view and we're biased against any information challenging it.

We all practice *mental accounting*, which is very different from actual accounting. In actual accounting, revenues from different sources are given the same values, as long as the values are actually the same. A dollar from the sale of a product would have the same value as a dollar from a lawsuit victory.

In mental accounting, we treat money differently, depending on its source. We're most careful with money we've earned through our own labors. The more we sacrifice for a dollar, the more careful we are in spending it and the more we expect in exchange for that dollar.

Money that's given to us by a known person is treated with less respect than money we earn ourselves. Children are more willing to freely spend money earned by their parents than money earned themselves. Money received as an inheritance is spent even more freely, especially if the benefactor wasn't close to the heir.

Money that's received from an anonymous source garners the least respect. Gambling winnings, whether from the state lottery or a hot weekend in Vegas, are more likely than any other revenues to be spent frivolously. Casinos are well aware of this tendency. They want you to win early and then slowly start losing your winnings back to them as the odds (which always favor the house) take effect. You're willing to lose your winnings because you're only gambling with "found" money. Of course, you keep on gambling (and losing) well past the point where your winnings are gone. The casino knows you'll end up gambling well after you're in the hole because they know of a human behavior you're now aware of – the sunk cost fallacy.

Even if you don't gamble, if you've never received an inheritance, and if every dollar you have you earned by the sweat of your brow and brain, you may still be guilty of mental accounting.

The source of a dollar can affect how we value that dollar. The volume of dollars can also affect the value we give to each one. The *law of marginal utility* is the term we give to the tendency to value something less as we get more of it. A $1,000 raise means far less to a person making $100,000 than it does to a person making $20,000.

If you've ever run low on gas on a lonely stretch of highway, you've experienced the law of marginal utility. You slowed down, turned off the A/C, and did everything possible to minimize fuel consumption until you found a gas station. Once you filled up and fuel was no longer a scarce commodity, you floored it to make up for lost time.

One of the dangers of cyber money is we don't see it or touch it; it therefore seems less real, less like money than currency we can see and hold and count. When you go shopping online, you can buy almost anything you want with just the click of a mouse. Spending money online doesn't feel like you're spending money, in part because you didn't forfeit cash in the purchase and because you may have to wait for the item to arrive. Two subsequent events will have very distinct and different feelings, though. The item will arrive, and it will feel like Christmas morning. The credit card bill will arrive shortly after, and it will feel like Good Friday.

Speaking of credit cards, they may be where most of us are guilty of mental accounting. When you purchase an item with cash, you have to actually open your wallet and hand over cash to the cashier (an almost archaic term now). There's an actual *exchange* that takes place. When you pay by credit card, you swipe your card and put it back in your wallet – there's no sense of loss, only gain, at least at that moment. That no-pain-only-gain illusion we get when we pay by credit card is one reason why people pay an average of 17% more for items that are purchased by credit card than the same items purchased with cash.

Mental accounting also includes being bad with fractions, at least denominators of fractions. Our focus is usually on the numerator.

It's the numerator we hear about on the evening news. The numerator is the person murdered, the multi-car accident, the drug bust, whatever will get your attention. We hear such stories and think the world is more dangerous than it is. We feel that way because we're focused on the numerator and ignoring the denominator.

We like to think that small towns are safer than big cities. I live in metropolitan Atlanta, with a population of over five million. My wife is from Sandersville, a small town in middle Georgia, with a population of about five thousand. Most people would think Sandersville would be the safer place to live, and there are certainly fewer total crimes committed (the numerator) in Sandersville than in metro Atlanta. However, Atlanta is *1,000 times* bigger than Sandersville, which means there has to be 1,000 times as many crimes here as there for us to be less safe than them. You have to look at the numerator and the denominator to get the whole picture.

Humans think in two different ways - one that's intuitive and automatic, the other that's rational and reflective. Psychologists refer to these methods of thinking as System 1 and System 2, respectively.

The automatic system is just that - it relies on instinct, rather than thought. When we react to a clap of thunder or a baby's laugh, we're using our automatic system. The reflective system is thoughtful and deliberate. I used my reflective system when writing this book, and you're using yours while reading it. Your native tongue is your automatic system regarding language. It takes years of training to take a second language from your reflective system to your automatic system. (One indicator that a second language is automatic is dreaming in that language.) The goal of almost any learned skill is to raise it to the level where the exercise of that skill goes from being reflective to automatic.

We prefer to use our automatic system because it's a lot less work than using our reflective system. We also like to give ourselves credit for using our reflective systems when we're actually using our automatic systems. When we watch TV news or read journals that agree with our point of view, we like to think we're being reflective, even though we are actually defaulting to our automatic systems. Reflective thinking involves *reflecting* on what the other side is saying, and that reflection requires some serious effort, as all reflective thinking does.

While humans aren't lazy, we're constantly seeking ways to perform a task with less effort. Most of man's inventions with moving parts are the result of this quest to do more work with less human effort. As part of this never-ending quest, any time we can move a task from our reflective to our automatic system, we're likely to do so.

Our habits are controlled by our automatic system. Our automatic system looks to make the everyday tasks of living as effortless as possible. The main reason we develop habits is so we don't have to think about what we're doing. Almost by definition, if you have to think about doing something, it isn't a habit. All those tasks you do in the course of a day - those that, once you've done them, you can't remember any of the specifics - are habits, and they're being handled by your automatic system.

Humans have an inherent mind-body conflict. Our bodies are built for performance, but our brains are always looking for ways to minimize energy consumption. Both body and brain have evolved this way over hundreds of thousands of years, and we won't change any time soon. As a species, humans are noteworthy for our physical endurance, but endurance depends on conserving energy, which is the brain's responsibility.

This mind-body conflict is apparent when we think about exercising. If you exercise regularly, it didn't come about naturally; you had to make a habit of it. Making a habit of regular exercise may not have reduced the physical energy required to exercise, but creating the habit of exercise practically eliminates the mental energy required to get started. When exercising isn't a habit, the hardest part of it is just getting started.

The irony of modern man is that the endurance our species developed over hundreds of thousands of years gave us the ability to hunt animals by literally running them to death. The protein-rich diet provided by hunting gave our brains the food it needed to grow. Now our brain undermines our endurance by telling us to conserve energy, even though we expend almost no energy on a daily basis, compared to our ancient forebears.

This irony is the product of a brain that can learn new things faster than it can unlearn old ones. For almost all of human history, taking it easy wasn't an option. Only in the last century or so have we created the technology that enables a large portion of the human population to support themselves while expending almost no physical energy and relatively little mental energy. For many of us, we must seek ways to consume energy through physical activity, and that practice goes against our instincts.

People become members of a church for two reasons: to strengthen their connection to God and to strengthen their connection to other people. It's not a coincidence that two of the most important committees in many churches are the worship and fellowship committees. These two committees have the task of making sure people get what they came for when they joined that church.

People who are involved in some form of organized religion have fewer health problems, fewer financial problems, longer lives, and higher measures of happiness than their non-religious counterparts. Some of these benefits are the result of trusting in a higher power to see them through life's crises. They're also the result of having a support system of people who can offer a helping hand, a pat on the back, and even a kick in the butt as the situation requires.

In the late nineteenth century, sociologist Emile Durkheim gathered data from across Europe to study factors that affected the suicide rate. No matter how Durkheim parsed the data, one fact never changed - the fewer social bonds, constraints, and obligations a person had, the higher the risk for suicide. People with the less demanding religious lives had higher suicide rates. People living alone were most likely to take their own life; married people, less; married people with children, still less.

A century of studies since Durkheim have confirmed his findings. Having strong *social networks* strengthens your immune system, extends life expectancy (even more than quitting smoking), speeds recovery from illness and injury, and reduces the risks of depression and anxiety disorders. If you want to be healthy, good friends may be the best medicine.

Animals with bigger brains have more complex social networks, and we humans are at the top of that list. We have large frontal lobes because we have the largest social groups. We have the largest social groups because we couldn't survive without them. The only way we survived as a species, much less came to dominate, was because of our ability to develop and maintain complex social networks.

Ambrose Bierce, the nineteenth century journalist, defined an acquaintance as "someone we know well enough to borrow from, but not well enough to lend to." Based on Bierce's definition, acquaintances never borrow from one another because no one is willing to be the lender. The networks of greatest value are those that are comprised of more than acquaintances. You need people you can borrow from, but more important, you need people you're willing to lend to.

These deeper relationship networks not only provide a sense of belonging and moral support, they also provide the opportunity to feel needed, which may be the most important benefit of all. When we get older, we often lose the connections that made us feel needed. One of the reasons why volunteerism is strongest among those over 65 is the need they have to still feel needed.

Our ability to establish and maintain relationships is limited. Anthropologists have calculated that, throughout human history, we tend to peak at about 150 when it comes to relationships that go beyond mere acquaintances. The similar pattern of relationships across humanity has led anthropologists to the *village theory*. This group of 150 or so individuals who comprise our significant relationships is our "village." These people may be spread out over time and space, but they're the group with whom almost all of our serious human interactions occur.

The best relationships are built on five attributes: respect, shared experience, mutual enjoyment of each other's company, trust, and reciprocity. The ability to establish and maintain all five of these attributes in a relationship is one reason why the number of meaningful relationships we can handle is limited. The importance of a relationship in our lives is also based largely on to what degree these five attributes are present.

As a social construct, *reciprocity* means that in response to friendly actions, people are frequently much nicer and much more cooperative than what could be expected by the self-interest model; conversely, in response to hostile actions, reciprocity is frequently much nastier and sometimes quite brutal. Reciprocity encompasses the concepts of the Golden Rule, mutual back scratching, quid pro quo, and an eye for an eye.

Reciprocity isn't the same as altruism or even gift giving. Altruism is helping those less fortunate, with the only reward being the positive feelings that result from the good deed. Gift giving is not typically based on need, but rather on the desire to make someone else happy.

Reciprocity is based both on the other party's intentions as well as the consequences of their actions. We actually feel a greater obligation to reciprocate when someone attempted to do us a favor that didn't work out than we do for someone who inadvertently benefitted us. Reciprocity is based on a trading of favors, as opposed to a formal negotiation or contract.

In addition to positive reciprocity, there's also negative reciprocity, which might be construed as retaliation or revenge. Negative reciprocity, unlike positive reciprocity, doesn't have the expectation of gain. Other than the pleasure of getting back at someone who has harmed you, the only other benefit to negative reciprocity may be to discourage such acts by the perpetrator or others in the future. In certain circles, such as the Mafia, to not retaliate when you've been wronged is taken as a sign of weakness and invites even worse abuses in the future.

One problem of reciprocity focuses on the unequal profit obtained from the concept of reciprocal concessions. Whether it's unsolicited address stickers in the mail from some charity or flowers passed out by a religious cult at the airport, people who want something from us know that the best way to get it is to give us something that is unsolicited (and of lower value) first, and then wait for the reciprocity gene to kick in before making their sales pitch. Without our instinct for reciprocity, free samples might cease to exist.

Reciprocity is part of more intimate relationships, too. Any relationship that has the potential to become more than a mere acquaintance is very sensitive to balance in the early stages. These relationships grow through a balance of give and take, such as gifts, favors, attention, and self-disclosure. Giving too much too early can make you seem needy or potentially exploiting. Giving too little can make you seem cold or selfish.

Most psychologists believe there are six basic human *emotions*: happiness, anger, fear, sadness, disgust, and surprise. All other emotions are varieties of these basic emotions. Each emotion is characterized by physiological and behavioral qualities, including those of movement, posture, voice, facial expression, and pulse rate fluctuation.

Plato believed that every human being actually has three souls:

- The *Rational* Soul is the thinking portion within each of us. It judges what's true and false and makes decisions based on the best way to properly live one's life. A properly functioning rational soul is the source of wisdom.
- The *Spirited* Soul is where certain emotions, including fear, dwell. It's the active portion, and its function is to carry out the dictates of the rational soul. A properly functioning spirited soul is the source of courage.
- The *Appetitive* Soul also contains emotions, including those responsible for the seven deadly sins. The desires and emotions of the appetitive soul must be controlled or deferred if we're to successfully achieve rational goals. A properly functioning appetitive soul is the source of moderation.

Plato stated the spirited soul puts into action the decisions of the rational soul, which assumes that action follows thought. Most people don't operate in this sequence, and virtually all bad decisions don't operate in this sequence. Plato viewed man as a rational being that will give sober thought to a problem, discern the best solution that benefits the most while harming the least, then act with courage to make that solution a reality. In reality, people act first on emotion and then attempt to justify what they've done by looking for any scrap of logic that will support their actions. We all do it to some degree, and we all do it to a higher degree than we recognize or admit.

One of the hallmarks of the present time is that people are encouraged to express their emotions. Expressing emotions is generally healthy, healthier than repressing them and letting the stress of repression lead to ulcers, migraines, and strokes.

There's a difference, however, between expressing emotions and surrendering to them. Emotions prompt us to action, but acting on our emotions is almost always bad in the long run. When we act on our emotions, we're usually trying to accomplish one of two things - create pleasure or avoid pain. Either of these powerful drives can lead us to hasty actions with adverse consequences.

One of the strongest human emotions is *fear*. Along with greed, fear is the emotion that most destroys a person's chances for financial success. (My book, *Whipsawed*, looks at the harmful effects of these two emotions.)

Fear has been an indispensable part of survival as long as there have been species on the planet equipped with brains, nervous systems, and senses. Fear is not unlike food as a survival tool – if you have too little or too much of either, your survival is in jeopardy. Too little fear exposes you to risks that can kill you. Too much fear prevents you from taking the risks necessary to survive, evolve, and prosper. The trick from the beginning of humankind has been to distinguish between fear that's harmful and fear that's helpful and to act only on fear that's helpful.

For thousands of years, the fears of humans weren't much different from the fears of other animal species. We feared overt threats like predators, harsh weather, injuries, and lack of food and water. As our brains developed, we increased our store of knowledge. We developed language to communicate with our fellow humans. As we got smarter, we increased our abilities to control many of the aspects of life that caused us fear. At the same time, as man developed technology, our lives became more complicated. As our lives became more complicated, the potential for something to go wrong became greater. Even as we worked to master the cause of our old fears, our growing brains and communication skills made it easier to create and share new fears.

Fear is typically experienced in anticipation of a specific pain or danger. Fear is also an uneasiness of the mind upon the thought of future evil likely to befall us. The first kind of fear is instinctual, the kind of fear we experience when we hear a sudden crash of thunder or step into the path of an oncoming vehicle. The second kind of fear, the kind that rolls around in one's mind, is very different.

The first kind of fear could be considered a healthy fear. Healthy fear is built into us as a survival mechanism. The second kind of fear is the one that's all in your head. This fear is the uneasiness of the *mind*; it's based on *thoughts* of potential future trouble. Fear that comes from our head is an unhealthy fear. Unhealthy fear is the kind that consumes our thoughts, paralyzes us, causes us to act irrationally, and possibly leads to phobias and paranoia.

In statistical analysis, there are Type I and Type II errors. A Type I error is also known as a *false positive*; a Type II error is known as a *false negative*. When we look at fear, a false positive can be thought of as believing something should be feared when it really shouldn't be. A false negative can be thought of as believing something shouldn't be feared when it really should be.

For ancient humans, a few false positives were better than even one false negative because the false negatives were almost always fatal. They also didn't have many false positives. Their lifestyle was primitive, but simple, so there were fewer things to trigger an irrational fear.

For modern humans, our lives are full of false negatives and false positives when it comes to fears. Which category predominates is often the result of conditions at the time. In good times, we have more false negatives. We feel safer and braver and are more likely to ignore or downplay a real danger. In bad times, we have more false positives. We're more likely to see danger where it doesn't exist, or at least to overestimate the danger of something.

Seven deadly sins, adaptation, loss aversion, hindsight bias, endowment effect, status quo bias, anchoring, framing, sunk-cost fallacy, remembrance, cognitive dissonance, confirmation bias, mental accounting, law of marginal utility, automatic/reflective systems, habits, mind-body conflict, village theory, reciprocity, false negatives/positives, emotions – these are just some of the many characteristics and behaviors humans have developed to help them exist in their world. Some are helpful and some are harmful, and some can be both, depending on the circumstances. What they all have in common is they developed as a way for humans to function in the secular world. One of the major challenges for humans seeking a greater understanding of the spiritual world is the need to transcend much of the humanness of our humanity.

WHAT YOU WANT ISN'T *REALLY* WHAT YOU WANT

DISAPPOINTMENT
WHEN THE VIRGINS THAT AWAIT YOU AREN'T QUITE WHAT YOU EXPECTED

Prior to the Industrial Revolution, material goods were hand-made, scarce, and expensive. Equally scarce were jobs that paid more than the barest subsistence wages. When it came to material possessions, people spent all their effort making what little they had last as long as it could. To provide one's family with the most basic necessities of food, clothing, and shelter was a major accomplishment well into the nineteenth century.

It's easy to forget that throughout almost all of human history, thrift was such a common trait that it wasn't thought of as a virtue along the lines of courage or charity. Thrift wasn't practiced as a repudiation of greed, nor as a method to accumulate wealth; it was a survival skill, as important as hunting and farming.

The Industrial Revolution provided the world with cheap goods and money to buy them. While the primary focus of the Industrial Revolution was to increase the *production* of goods, its greatest impact on mankind has been the increased *consumption* of goods, with all its side-effects.

The Industrial Revolution and the Consumer Age it spawned changed mankind more than anything since the transition from B.C. to A.D. Traditions based on family and community gave way to "improvement" of the individual's position. Desires, which were previously considered an emotion to be controlled, were now encouraged. It's no coincidence that advertising first appeared during the same period that the Industrial Revolution made consumer goods more plentiful.

Personal vices became the catalyst for public prosperity. Avarice, pride, envy, and greed fueled the Industrial Revolution as much as coal and steam did. Being a consumer had previously carried negative connotations, and being called a consumer was not a compliment. Even today, dictionary definitions of such words as *consumer* and *consumption* include terms like *waste*, *destroy*, and *squander*.

Ironically, even as consumption was being redefined from a fulfillment of needs to a satisfaction of desires, the connotations associated with consumption changed from vice to virtue. As we morphed into a consumer-based economy, to be a voracious consumer went from being anti-social to being, at least occasionally, patriotic.

If you're an American old enough to be reading this book, you've been exposed to hundreds of thousands, if not millions of messages telling you what you're supposed to want. Almost all of them had a connection to money. Either you were told to want something that costs money, or, and this is even more corrupting, you were told to want money for its own sake.

When it comes to money and the role it plays in our wants, what we should really want is to minimize the effects that changes in our financial condition have in our overall well-being and happiness. Sudden wealth shouldn't cause a change in who we are, what our priorities are, or how we treat other human beings. A financial setback, even one that may wipe us out financially, should make us realize that all we've lost is money. The qualities we possess that are priceless will enable us to replace lost wealth. Financial setbacks can even serve a purpose if they help us refocus on what is of real value, including what makes us valuable as a person.

If you don't believe we have something in common with monkeys, here's food for thought. In Southeast Asia for centuries there's been an effective way to capture monkeys, especially macaques. These monkeys are occasionally captured for amusement, but more often are killed by farmers because they're considered pests. A large coconut is used, and a hole about an inch and a half in diameter is bored into it. After the milk is drained, fruits and nuts that are attractive to the monkey are inserted into the coconut through the hole. The coconut is then placed in an area where it can be observed.

Before long a monkey gets the scent of the coconut's contents and checks it out. The monkey inserts its hand into the coconut and grabs a handful of the culinary delights. Here's the problem – while the monkey's hand can fit into the hole, the monkey's fist, especially when it's filled with food, cannot be pulled out of the coconut.

At this point a human saunters up and throws a net over the monkey, and the monkey's fate is sealed.

You're probably wondering why the monkey wouldn't just let go of the food, remove its hand from the coconut the same way it went in, and escape. For some reason, either the monkeys don't recognize the coconut is a trap or (and this is where they act human) they can't bear to relinquish a material good, even when retaining it puts them in great danger.

One kind of trap is that which keeps us hanging on to something when hanging on will harm us. Another trap is the consuming desire for something we don't own.

In Greek mythology, Tantalus was a son of Zeus and therefore enjoyed a great many privileges. Despite such privileges, Tantalus fell victim to envy and greed, leading him to steal ambrosia and nectar from Zeus' table. He brought them back to his kingdom and revealed the secrets of the gods.

For his punishment, Tantalus was forced to stand in a pool of water with the branches of a fruit tree hanging just overhead. Whenever he reached for the fruit, the branches receded just out of reach. Whenever he bent down to take a drink, the water receded before he could get any. Tantalus was cursed with eternal deprivation of nourishment. The word *tantalize*, defined as temptation without satisfaction, is taken from this tragic figure of Greek mythology.

While none of us are guilty of stealing nectar from the gods, we may feel like Tantalus at times. Whenever a commercial enterprise runs advertising for a product that's totally out of the price range for the great majority of its audience, they're tantalizing those people. The creation of desire, which is the entire purpose of advertising, is nothing but tantalization to those who have no hope of ever fulfilling such desires.

When asked to define happiness, we often struggle to answer. Psychologist Ed Diener says that happiness is not a desirable set of life circumstances; it's a way of traveling. Diener conducted studies verifying that college students who were cheerful in college earned 30% more than their peers after twenty years. Being cheerful boosts earnings more than attending a top university does. While being financially successful may increase happiness, Diener's study indicates that happiness is more likely to lead to financial success. Happiness is desirable for its own sake, but it also offers financial benefits as well.

While money and happiness are far from the only areas where we confuse cause and effect, it's perhaps the most important area because of the importance that both money and happiness play in our lives. Too many of us spend our lives thinking money will bring happiness. In reality, happiness will likely bring money; the odds are certainly better for the latter than the former. One of comedian Henny Youngman's most famous quips was, "What good is happiness? It can't buy money." Based on Dr. Diener's findings, apparently it can.

Abraham Lincoln said that people are as happy or unhappy as they choose to be. While we certainly have some control over our level of happiness, it's worth recognizing the genetic factors involved.

Happiness is one of the most highly heritable aspects of personality. Studies of twins show from 50 to 80% of all the variance among people in their average levels of happiness can be explained by genetics rather than life experiences. Your DNA may have something to say about your upper and lower limits of happiness, but our happiness level within that range is under our control.

In some ways, the path to happiness requires us to swim against the current of evolution. Because we evolved to respond more strongly to threats than to opportunities as a survival mechanism, we see too many things as bad and not enough as good. We react to bad things more strongly, quickly, and persistently than equivalent good things. If we've evolved to first see the bad in a situation, seeing the good and creating happiness requires us to fight instinct and to be counterintuitive.

Adverse fortune could hardly be considered a source of happiness, but it can serve to help us see the true sources of happiness more clearly. Adverse fortune is more beneficial than good fortune. Good fortune rarely makes us grateful; it only makes us greedy for more. Adverse fortune makes us strong – and humble.

Albert Schweitzer, philosopher, physician, missionary, and recipient of the Nobel Peace Prize, said, "Success is not the key to happiness; happiness is the key to success." Dale Carnegie, author of one of the best-selling books of all time, *How to Win Friends and Influence People*, said, "Success is getting what you want; happiness is wanting what you get." These two quotations point out two important points about happiness. First, happiness can be both a starting point *and* a destination. Second, happiness is not something we find; it's something we create.

There's hardly a soul alive who hasn't said, at some point, words to the effect: "If I only had (fill-in-the-blank), I'd be happy." We begin such thinking in childhood. We all just knew that if we got that special gift from Santa, our world would be perfect, and we'd experience perfect and eternal happiness. Santa granted our wish, but by the time the twelfth day of Christmas rolled around, we were already bored with our special gift. As adults, many of us have sought happiness in places like auto showrooms. We spend way more than we should to buy a vehicle that quickly goes from chariot of the gods to mere conveyance to monthly marauder of our checking account.

When we think of taking on a challenge, it's natural to think in terms of success and failure. Success and failure should be thought of as nouns describing outcomes, not as adjectives describing persons.

Success and failure have an emotional connection because two of our most powerful emotions are linked closely to them - success with happiness and failure with sadness. We naturally assume that when we're successful at something, happiness will immediately ensue. We also expect failure to bring sadness.

Because it's easier to generate negative emotions than positive ones and because we expect to feel sad when we fail, our expectations of sadness are almost always met. Ironically, one of the keys to success is to not let failure sadden you to the point of becoming discouraged. People like Thomas Edison failed far more often than they succeeded, yet ultimately such people are hailed as being extremely successful.

People equate success with happiness, and they often use the terms synonymously. Achieving success can often prove disappointing, though. A young woman may have a goal of reaching a certain management level at work. She may work long hours and make many sacrifices to climb the corporate ladder. Once the big promotion finally is received, she may experience more emptiness than elation. She may have the title, the salary, and the corner office. However, the rush of happiness she was expecting as part of the package isn't there because, contrary to popular expectations, happiness is not standard equipment on success. Also, because happiness didn't come automatically, she can be left feeling not merely neutral but sad because her expectations were so unmet.

This young woman may be surprised by her is-that-all-there-is? syndrome, but she's hardly unique. Singer Peggy Lee had a hit song in 1969 titled *Is That All There Is?*, which itself was inspired by a story written 75 years earlier by German writer Thomas Mann. Both dealt with the disappointment that comes with getting what you wanted and finding it isn't what you expected.

Success and failure are travelling companions. As you journey toward a goal, you'll inevitably encounter both along the way. Harvard business professor Rosabeth Moss Kanter, who has studied many business organizations, observed: "Everything can look like failure in the middle. If you understand that failures along the way are an inevitable part of long-term success and if that recognition enables you to control the negative emotions that come along with those failures, you are much more likely to persevere to the point of eventual success."

When we begin a new challenge, we start out with many positive emotions - hope being perhaps the strongest of them all. Hope is an essential emotion in getting any project off the ground, but as Sir Francis Bacon observed, "Hope is a good breakfast, but it is a poor supper." Once the initial excitement at the beginning of the journey has waned and the long slog toward the finish line is all there is at the moment, we can become like kids in the back seat on a long drive - "Are we there yet? Are we there yet?"

Knowing we'll face valleys along the way to our goals can actually make us optimistic. Knowing that failure is going to cross our path on the journey to success, we're more likely to seek it out and confront it, rather than fearing and avoiding it. It isn't the obstacle that we choose to face head-on that defeats us; it's the object that blindsides us because we refuse to acknowledge it.

When a goal comes closer to realization, our emotions improve, with confidence of success leading the way. There's a U-shape to the emotional pattern we encounter when we work toward a long-term goal - hope and anticipation at the beginning, confidence and pride toward the end, but a cornucopia of negative emotions in the middle, including but not limited to, anger, cynicism, depression, despair, impatience, stress, and uncertainty.

People whose goal is perfection in every decision are known as *maximizers*. Maximizers tend to be frustrated and unhappy because reality almost never meets their goals and expectations. They'll spend a great deal of time on the decision-making process, and they'll make some excellent decisions as a result. Unfortunately, they'll never fully enjoy the fruits of their labors because their assessment is based on relative standards, not absolute ones. Their assessment is based relative to perfection, which is impossible to achieve.

Satisficers are the opposite of maximizers. They don't expect perfection from themselves, and they don't expect their decisions to be perfect. Satisficers set absolute standards, and when those standards have been met, they don't spend additional resources for incremental improvements. Satisficers are well aware of the point of diminishing returns, whereas maximizers blow way past that point because they're obsessed with perfection.

Maximizers may make some better individual decisions than satisficers, but they also don't make some decisions that need to be made. They're preoccupied with making the best decision every time. Satisficers may give up a little on the quality of their decisions, but they more than make up for it in quantity. Satisficers will take care of all the business that needs to be taken care of and will still have a life. While the pursuit of perfection can be noble, expecting to ever reach it is a guarantee of unhappiness.

Maximizers engage in more social comparison and are more easily drawn into conspicuous consumption. Conspicuous consumption refers to things that are visible to others and are used as a marker of a person's relative success. These goods derive their value not from objective properties but from the statement they make about their owner. The goods that move someone up the ladder devalue the possessions of others. Because we're far more attuned to changes in conditions than we are in absolute levels, people who focus on relative position, such as maximizers, are negatively affected by a relative change in position, even if their absolute position improves.

Comparing our situation to others is likely to lead to unhappiness, regardless of our absolute position. The natural tendency is to compare to those better off, which generates negative feelings. We compare ourselves to those worse off and feel gratitude far less frequently.

As an illustration of how comparisons can affect our feeling of happiness, consider Cornelius Vanderbilt. Vanderbilt was one of the first railroad tycoons of the

19th century. He was instrumental in the formation of his namesake, Vanderbilt University. He built Grand Central Station. When he died in 1877 at age 82, his fortune was estimated at $100 million. He is considered the third richest man in American history after John D. Rockefeller and Andrew Carnegie.

The poor today are likely to feel unhappy when they look at their position relative to the rest of America. However, of those classified as poor today, 99% have electricity, running water, a refrigerator, and flush toilets; 97% have a television and a telephone; 78% have a car and air conditioning. The middle-class of 1955 would be described as below-the-poverty-line today because they lacked most of the amenities the poor have today. When you consider the above list of items that the poor have today, items that most middle-class Americans didn't have in 1955, consider one more thing - Cornelius Vanderbilt had none of these. The poor in America today still have more than most Americans did in the Eisenhower era, and they have access to hundreds of inventions and discoveries that didn't exist in the so-called Gilded Age of the Rockefellers and Vanderbilts.

Pursuing wealth and prestige in the search for happiness will usually backfire. People who report the greatest interest in attaining money and fame are consistently less happy and less healthy than those who pursue less materialistic goals. As I said previously, money is not the cause; it is the effect. In the case of someone like Cornelius Vanderbilt, his sense of achievement was in building a railroad empire, not in amassing a fortune.

The *nucleus accumbens* is one of the oldest and most primitive parts of the human brain. It's sometimes referred to as the pleasure center. The highs that are experienced from sex, drugs, gambling, etc. all originate in the nucleus accumbens. The highs that come from acquisition and accumulation also originate there.

When a pleasurable sensation stimulates the nucleus accumbens, it releases the chemical *dopamine*. Dopamine is the reason we feel that feeling of contentment/ecstasy. It isn't the act itself that creates a physically pleasurable experience; it's the release of the dopamine triggered by the pleasurable experience that does it for us. Seeking pleasure is one of the first programs God installed in the human brain. He wants us to have pleasures; He just doesn't want us to be ruled by pleasures.

Pleasure is a sensual gratification or indulgence. Pleasure is the result of an external stimulus. In America, there are so many pleasure stimuli promising to give happiness that it's easy to be misled. Most people who are seeking happiness make a wrong turn and look for it down the path of pleasure. Sex, drugs, rock 'n roll, a new Mercedes, a house at the beach, and a Mediterranean vacation can all bring pleasure; none of them can bring happiness.

There's a difference between pleasure and gratification and between pleasure and happiness. According to psychologist Martin Seligman, one of the premier experts on happiness, pleasures are, "…delights that have clear sensory and strong emotional components", like one gets from food and sex. Gratifications are activities that engage you fully, draw on your strengths, and allow you to become less self-conscious. Gratification leads to *flow*. Gratification is positive reinforcement that makes you want to continue doing something.

When we're deriving pleasure from working toward a goal, we're said to be in a state of flow. When we enter a state of flow, hard work becomes effortless. We want to keep exerting ourselves, honing our skills, using our strengths, accomplishing, learning, improving, feeling challenged. This effort leads to gratification. The successful *achievement* becomes a byproduct of the joy we get from the *act of achieving* and less a goal itself.

There's often more pleasure in the progress toward a goal than in the actual achievement, which is one reason why achieving a goal can trigger disappointment. As Shakespeare said, "Joy's soul lies in the doing." In my case, while I enjoy completing a book I'm writing, I often enjoy the process of writing it even more. When we're progressing toward a goal, part of the enjoyment is the anticipation of reaching the goal. And, as in many of life's events, the fulfillment has a hard time matching the anticipation.

A habit can be labeled "bad" for more reasons than harming one's physical, mental, or financial health. People's bad habits may give them pleasure, but they don't make them happy. Happiness involves a holistic experience, which means happiness depends on the total effect of an activity. A bad habit, like smoking or overeating, may bring pleasure at the moment of consumption, but the overall effect is to make the user unhappy, because the overall effect is negative. Happiness isn't generated from a negative.

Pleasure is externally generated; happiness is internally generated, which is why pleasure can't substitute for happiness. Happiness is an "inside job". It doesn't depend on external circumstances or material wealth for its existence and growth. While it's easy to overindulge in activities that bring pleasure, there's no such thing as too much of something that brings true happiness. Happiness leaves no hangovers.

If you're looking to obtain happiness by spending money, there's a right way and wrong way to do it. The right way is to buy experiences. The wrong way is to buy stuff. Expensive activities tend to be done with other people, while expensive possessions tend to be purchased, at least in part, to impress other people. Part of the joy of travelling to foreign countries is creating pleasurable memories, sharing the experience with friends and family, and making new friends on the trip. The pleasure of an expensive car is derived largely on showing it off, rather than strictly the pleasure of the driving experience.

Despite one of the highest standards of living in the world, Americans are not measurably happier than those in other countries. We're happier than the citizens of Egypt, but not of Mexico. Our inability to find happiness through our standard of living is one of many factors contributing to increased levels of depression.

Psychologist Martin Seligman has a four-step theory on the rise in depression:

- Individualism – If your life is based on pure individualism and something goes poorly, there's no counterweight, such as a religious community. Nothing can pull you in the right direction.
- Self-Esteem Craze – It's unrealistic to expect to feel good about yourself all the time. Real self-esteem is also based on actual accomplishments, not mere existence.
- Victim Mentality – Despite personal freedoms that have never been higher, the victim mentality deters people from exerting control over their psyches.

- Consumerism – Spending is seen as a short-cut to happiness. While run-away consumerism may bring short-term pleasure, its financial toll brings long-term unhappiness.

Consumer satisfaction and dissatisfaction depend less on what a person has in an absolute sense and more on what they have compared to their chosen reference group. Although media promotion of conspicuous consumption is justly criticized, the most powerful stimulator of desire is what friends, family, and peers have.

People acquire status goods with the expectation that others will imbue greater status because of their possession of those status goods. Possessions fulfill an important function of orienting us in our social worlds. When we view the possessions of someone, we form impressions and calculate how to interact with them. For example, researchers have discovered that people wait longer to honk at someone lingering at a green light if that person is driving a prestige automobile. We have a natural tendency to defer to those with greater wealth, or at least the appearance of greater wealth.

Similar to loss aversion in investing, *fear of falling* is a real condition for people caught in a spending spiral. The perceived penalties for lowering spending, lower status being the most prominent, are frightening enough to cause people to keep spending well beyond their means. The desire for prestige trumps the need for financial stability.

As we climb the socio-economic ladder, we change our reference group, causing us to spend more to keep up with our peers. But upscaling is socially irrational. The goal is to seem better off, compared to others.

However, if everyone else is also spending too much to move upscale, the relative positions don't change. It's akin to everyone standing up at a sporting event. No one is better off in comparison to others, but everyone's worse off compared to when they were all sitting.

The millionaires cited in *The Millionaire Next Door* are millionaires precisely because they haven't changed their reference groups when it comes to spending. They prefer to be thought poor while being rich than to be thought rich while being poor. Financial independence is far more important than status to those millionaires.

A sense of financial security largely emerges from how a person appraises three basic gaps in their lives: the gap between what one has and what one wants, the gap between what one has and what one thinks others have, and the gap between what one has and the best one has had in the past. The larger the gap(s), the greater is one's financial insecurity.

One's sense of financial security can therefore be enhanced in several ways. Closing the gap between what one has and what one wants can be done by simply wanting less, which can be done largely by being grateful and content with what one already has. Closing the gap between what one has and what one thinks others have can be done by recognizing that boasting is easier than confessing. People are happy to show off their assets, but they go to great pains to hide their liabilities. Closing the gap between what one has and the best they had in the past may be more difficult because we can't change the past, and changing our present condition may not be possible in the short run. A reappraisal of the past might be helpful, which should include a hard look at the negatives of the past position.

University of California professor of psychology Sonja Lyubomirsky is a recognized expert on what makes people happy or unhappy. In her research, she has developed a subjective happiness scale, which enables someone to determine his/her chronic level of happiness. From this scale a person can be categorized as relatively happy or unhappy. One of the most interesting findings of Dr. Lyubomirsky's studies is how happy and unhappy people react differently if they compare themselves to others.

When working with a peer on a project, happy people were only slightly affected by their performance relative to a peer. If they did better than their peer, they felt slightly better about their performance. If they did worse than their peer, it did not affect whether the person felt good about his/her performance. The happy person could still appreciate an improvement in the performance of a task, even if someone else performed better.

Unhappy people, by contrast, did not feel better about an improved performance if a peer had a better performance. Unhappy people were too busy comparing themselves to their peers, instead of to their own previous performance. Happy people focused almost exclusively on how they compared to themselves, not how they compared to others.

Unhappy people also had their moods worsen if a peer got more positive feedback from a performance, even if that unhappy person got positive feedback as well. Their whole mood was based on how they compared to someone else. They actually felt better about negative feedback if the peer's feedback were more negative than they felt about positive feedback if the peer's feedback were more positive. The takeaway from these studies is that unhappy people spend a lot of time comparing themselves to other people, which is a big reason why they're unhappy. The happy people realize that the only person they have to be better than is the person they are right now.

Most of our life's goals fall into one of four categories: work and achievement, relationships and intimacy, religion and spirituality, and generativity (leaving a legacy and contributing to society). People who only have goals in the first category are less happy, on average, than those who strive in the other categories.

Humans were shaped by evolution to pursue success, not happiness. Much of human history involved zero-sum competition, and winning such competitions also won prestige. But success brings no lasting pleasure while raising the bar for future successes.

One of the questions on the financial questionnaire that my prospective clients complete asks them what they see as their mission(s) going forward. This may seem like an unusual question for the type of questionnaire that typically focuses on income, expenses, assets, and liabilities. That information is also requested, but the reason I ask about their missions is their answers tell me *what the money is for*.

By contemplating and answering a question about their missions, prospective clients are telling me what's most important for them to accomplish in the future. It's a way of telling me what they want most in whatever time they have left. This contemplation of their mission gives these people the opportunity to prioritize, which is essential since none of us can have everything we want. Typically, this prioritization puts things like proper health care, education for descendants, and financial independence ahead of things like vacation homes, new cars, and cruises. I also learn what I need to focus on with a particular client to do my job properly.

From my perspective as their financial advisor, it's essential I know what the money is for. Unless I know what the money is for, I'll never know when there's *enough money*. One of my cardinal rules of investing is we never take on any more risk than is necessary to achieve the client's mission. If there's no stated mission, there's no way to gauge the upper limit on risk. No upper limit on risk is a sure-fire recipe for disaster.

Occasionally, a prospective client will balk at the idea of stating a mission – any mission. In conjunction with that refusal, they may also tell me that what they use the money for is not my concern; my concern should only be maximizing the return on their money. What these people don't understand is, without knowing what the money is for and how much will be needed, no amount of money will ever be enough for them. More specifically, nothing I do for them on the investment front will ever satisfy them. Whatever they get, they'll always want *more*, and they'll frustrate themselves and anyone they work with in the fruitless quest for more.

One more thing – stating one's mission creates a much sharper focus. Now everyone – the clients, their families, their advisors – all know what we're working to accomplish. Distractions and detours will become far less prevalent. Staying the course during tough times will be far easier because there's a clear reason for staying the course. Success is far more likely and will be the kind that can actually generate happiness.

Conservative writer George Will says that Americans define a need as a 48-hour old want. Needs connote necessity. By claiming to need something, one avoids being viewed as overly ambitious or selfish. An established need signifies a right, a claim to something. Elevating a want to a need enables claiming without condemnation. The difference between want and need is the difference between *desire* and *require*.

The premise of all economics is that all of mankind's desires cannot be satisfied with all available resources. This scarcity of resources and the allocation of those resources exemplify the field of economics. The Christian perspective on needs and consumption is that God provides enough for all to live in abundance. That perspective clashes with economic theory, which states that there *isn't* enough for all to live in abundance, therefore choices have to be made.

Resolving the conflict between the Christian perspective and economic theory requires two things. First, there needs to be a definition of abundance. At a minimum, abundance should be defined as exceeding one's needs. Beyond that, there will be disagreements about what constitutes abundance. Second, regardless of the standard set for abundance, there's nothing to stop people from wanting even more. No amount of abundance ever annihilated avarice.

From Karl Marx: "The hoarding drive is boundless in nature. Money is independent of all limits. It is the universal representative of material wealth because it is directly convertible into any other commodity. The qualitative lack of limitation of money keeps driving the hoarder back to his Sisyphean task: accumulation. He is in the same situation as a world conqueror who discovers a new boundary with each country he annexes."

If you've ever known an avid collector, you've likely seen how the desire to increase their collection can become insatiable. As long as there are more examples out there to add to the collection, the collector feels compelled to go after them.

It's far worse with money because there's literally no limitation to how much one can collect. There are no storage issues – most of it is just numbers in account ledgers. There's also no point where the money collector says, "I'll stop now; I have enough." Virtually every human being who set a monetary accumulation goal and reached it immediately set a new, higher goal. As Marx said, there's always a new boundary to cross.

In his 1941 book *Escape from Freedom*, social theorist Erich Fromm argues that freedom is composed of two complementary parts - freedom *from* and freedom *to*. True freedom requires both, though each individual and culture may put greater emphasis on one over the other. We want to believe we have the freedom to choose, even if we make bad choices. We also want the freedom from the consequences of the bad choices of others. This tension is constant in any free society.

The cornerstone of American culture is choice. Freedom to choose and an abundance of choices draw people to America. The power of choice isn't just the means to an end but something intrinsically valuable and necessary. However, choice can become an imperative rather than an opportunity.

Modern individuals aren't merely *free* to choose, but are *obliged* to choose freely. Our choices are a reflection of who we are. The more choices we have, the more work we have to do to create who we are, and the greater the chance of making mistakes along the way. We generally choose in ways that make us stand out from the majority, but not in ways that make us part of a glaring and lonely minority. We want to be noticed, but not "gawked at".

When making a choice, do you think in terms of "I" or in terms of "we"? Different cultures have different emphases; the U.S. focuses almost exclusively on the "I". More collectivist societies, such as Japan, focus on the "we". Collectivist societies view their lives more in terms of duties than in personal preferences. The more homogeneous the population, the easier and more likely they are to think in terms of "we".

Greater wealth is associated with individualism. Higher population density is associated with collectivism. Higher education and greater exposure to other cultures are both associated with individualism.

A love marriage is an individualist endeavor; an arranged marriage is quintessentially collectivist. Love marriages increased with the rise of individualism in western society during the Middle Ages. The traditional wedding vows were first published in the Book of Common Prayer in 1549.

In arranged marriages, happiness is measured primarily by the fulfillment of duties; in love marriages, it's measured by the intensity and duration of the emotional connection. Love marriages tend to start out hot and cool over time, while arranged marriages start out cool and warm up over time, as the bride and groom grow to know and love each other.

If we want to maintain a high number of alternatives, we pay a price in time, sanity, and the bottom line. When people are given a moderate number of options (4 to 6) rather than a large number (20 to 30), they're more likely to make a choice, are more confident in their decisions, and are happier with what they choose.

It's often best to rely on the recommendations of an expert, provided the expert has your best interests in mind. Patients seem to respond best when they're made aware of the treatment options, but also get a clear recommendation from the doctor on the preferred treatment. It allows for choice while relieving the patient of total responsibility for the decision.

Edward Deci and Richard Ryan at the University of Rochester developed *Self-determination theory*, which states that humans have three innate psychological needs – competence, autonomy, and relatedness. When those needs are met, we're motivated, productive, and happy.

Competence is performing a task at a high level. Autonomy is freedom; control is the lack of it. Control leads to compliance; autonomy leads to engagement. Relatedness is seeing how our task fits into the larger scheme of things.

Higher tangible rewards more often lead to worse performance because they have a negative effect on intrinsic motivation. If-Then rewards (if you do this, then you'll get that) require people to forfeit some autonomy and can act as disincentives.

Self-set goals that involve mastery are healthy; imposed goals tend to have negative side effects. Intrinsic motivation minimizes unethical actions because the person who suffers most is you. Extrinsic rewards can almost force people onto the low road. Cheating almost always occurs when standards of performance are set by someone other than the performer.

Setting goals that are especially difficult to attain can be a recipe for frustration and dissatisfaction. Goals should be difficult enough that they offer a real challenge, but they shouldn't be so difficult to achieve that the price exceeds the prize. A series of step-by-step goals may serve one's purpose better than one humungous goal.

Hope for riches and fear of poverty have always gripped us, leading us to buy in hope and sell in fear. As a rule, men want freedom to strive for riches, while women want freedom from poverty. The more conscientious people are, the less they hope for riches and the more they desire freedom from poverty, which may explain why 90% of scam victims are men.

A study in *Quarterly Journal of Economics* looked at trading activity of 35,000 households. They found that:

- Men trade more often than women.
- Single men trade less sensibly than married men.
- Married men trade less sensibly than single women.
- The less the female presence, the less rational is the approach to trading in the markets.

Men want to believe that they're rational and that women are emotional, but when it comes to investing, the opposite is actually true.

Hope and fear affect the way we evaluate alternatives. With fear, we look at possibilities from the bottom up and wonder how bad things might get. The bottom up perspective emphasizes security. With hope, we look at possibilities from the top down and wonder how good things might get. The top down perspective emphasizes opportunity. Optimists have an abundance of hope; pessimists have an abundance of fear.

Present needs are felt through emotion. Future needs are recognized through thought. We feel present needs, but have to think about future needs. Feelings, unlike thoughts, require no effort, so future needs too often get shortchanged.

In the battle between present needs and future needs, present needs will always prevail. As long as present needs are truly needs, this is how it should be. After all, to get to the future, you have to survive the present, which requires your present needs be met.

The problem for many people begins when they start converting present wants into needs and then fulfill those wants at the expense of compromising their ability to meet future needs. Every time someone says they "need" a vacation, a new car, or a new wardrobe when they're not adequately saving for retirement, they're putting a present want ahead of a future need. Relabeling the want as a need won't ease the pain to come when they're unable to meet that future need.

One of the most common reasons people give for changing churches is: "My needs aren't being met." Many churches, especially some of the larger ones, market themselves as a place where one can have those needs met. But the point of the gospel is not simply to have our needs met, but to have our needs met so that we can meet the needs of others. When the church represents itself as merely a place where people can have their needs met, it robs them of the right to the joy of their own ministry. One of our most basic needs is to be needed. Any church that doesn't make its members feel needed in service to others in need is failing in one of its most important missions.

In his book, *Death by Suburb*, David L. Goetz notes that religion in the suburbs is more a program to join than something that changes your life. He offers some guidance for those with misguided expectations of their church:

- Making time or space for God is the most basic element of spirituality.
- True spirituality is the opposite of control.

- There's no way to the presence of Jesus without the dying to self and ceasing the quest for immortality symbols.
- There's no greater bondage than living only for what I don't yet have.
- Focus not on the possessions of those above me, but on the humanity of those below me.
- The more we try to control life, the more it controls us.
- Pursue action without worrying about results.
- When you thirst for more of Jesus, find a hopeless case or a hopeless cause.
- Freedom often means staying instead of going.

One of the most important books of the 20th Century was *Man's Search for Meaning*, by Viktor Frankl. Frankl was an up-and-coming psychiatrist in Vienna in the late 1930s. He was also Jewish, and his punishment for being Jewish was to be sent to Auschwitz and later Dachau concentration camps. Viktor Frankl's wife, mother, and brother died in the concentration camps – he and his sister were the only family members to survive the Holocaust.

Man's Search for Meaning offers two important perspectives. It serves as a journal and recollection of the daily life in the concentration camps from the perspective of a trained psychologist. It also offers insight into what is most important in life, which too often only becomes clear after great loss.

Here are some of Frankl's perspectives on what we should really want in life:

- Life is not a quest for pleasure or power, but a quest for meaning.
- There are three possible sources for meaning: in work, in love, and in courage during difficult times.

- The way in which a man accepts his fate and all the suffering it entails, the way in which *he takes up his cross*, gives him ample opportunity – even under the most difficult circumstances – to add a deeper meaning to his life.
- It did not really matter what we expected from life, but rather what life expected from us. Our answer must consist, not in talk and meditation, but in right action and in right conduct.
- Woe to him who, when the day of his dreams finally came, found it so different from all he had longed for!
- The crowning experience of all, for the homecoming man, is the wonderful feeling that, after all he has suffered, there is nothing he need fear any more – except his God.
- Sometimes the frustrated will to meaning is vicariously compensated for by a will to power, including the most primitive form of the will to power, the will to money.
- Suffering ceases to be suffering at the moment it finds a meaning, such as the meaning of a sacrifice.
- Pleasure is, and must remain, a side-effect or byproduct, and is destroyed and spoiled to the degree to which it is made a goal in itself.
- A human being is not one in pursuit of happiness, but rather in search of a reason to become happy.
- I understood how a man who has nothing left in this world still may know bliss, be it only for a brief moment, in the contemplation of his beloved.

Frankl also drew heavily on the words of Friedrich Nietzsche, a 19th century German philosopher, who said, "He who has a *why* to live can bear almost any *how*."

One reason what we want isn't *really* what we want is because we never stop to seriously contemplate *why* we want it. If we analyze the reasons we want something and if we're honest with ourselves, the answers too often look like these:

- It will convey status.
- It will inspire envy.
- It will make me immortal.
- It will make me look smarter/prettier/wealthier.
- It will give me power.
- It will fill a gap in my life.
- Advertising told me I wanted it.
- I don't have it already.
- I'll be the first kid on my block to have one.

Asking *why* about anything is probably the most important question to ask and the most difficult to answer. A *why* question requires an essay answer, not fill-in-the-blank. It requires thought, something we tend to do too little of when it comes to the things we want.

Asking ourselves why we want something before we pursue it is perhaps the best way to pursue more of what will help us, less of what will harm us, and it will bring us lasting happiness, rather than fleeting pleasure or even disappointment when it's finally attained.

WE'RE ALL STEWARDS... AND NOTHING MORE

When I was sixteen, our family took a trip to Toronto to visit relatives. They lived in a row house that had been built around 1900. The lots were very small, and the homes were modest. The neighborhood was old, but safe. I was comfortable walking alone at night in that neighborhood in a way that would never have been comfortable in a comparable American city at that time. The neighborhood was ethnically diverse, and people mingled with each other on the streets day and night.

One morning I awoke at dawn and went out on the small front porch. Across the narrow street I saw an old man of about eighty, neatly dressed with jet black hair that hadn't been his natural color for at least twenty years. The man was sweeping in front of his house. He wasn't sweeping his porch, his sidewalk, or even the sidewalk in front of his house. He was sweeping the *street* in front of his house. I watched him for a few minutes as he meticulously collected the dust and dirt that I couldn't even spot from across the street. My curiosity finally got the better of me, and I went over to ask him why he was sweeping the street; it certainly wasn't his responsibility, I said. He gave me that smile only wisdom confers, and he told me in his heavy Italian accent, "I sweep here because I live here."

In that one sentence I understood why this neighborhood was vibrant, with safe streets and well-maintained homes, and not a crime-ridden decaying slum like so many of its American counterparts. The residents, old and young alike, took responsibility for where they live. They didn't just maintain their homes, which they did to an astonishingly high degree. They took care of the neighborhood. They swept the streets. If something got broken, they fixed it immediately, without debating whose responsibility it was. It was *their* neighborhood, so it was *their* responsibility. Had there been graffiti, it would have been cleaned up before the paint could dry. However, I never saw any graffiti because people who love their home like this would never deface it. They were owners of their homes; they were also stewards of their neighborhood. Their stewardship was the reason the neighborhood was clean and safe and why their home values were high.

The broken windows theory was first introduced by social scientists James Q. Wilson and George L. Kelling, in an article titled "Broken Windows", which appeared in the March 1982 edition of *The Atlantic Monthly*. The title comes from the following example:

"Consider a building with a few broken windows. If the windows are not repaired, the tendency is for vandals to break a few more windows. Eventually, they may even break into the building, and if it's unoccupied, perhaps become squatters or light fires inside."

A successful strategy for preventing vandalism is to fix the problems while they're still small. Repair the broken windows within a short time, and vandals are much less likely to break more windows or do further damage. In other words, demonstrating good stewardship discourages others from mistreating what is not theirs. This is the behavior I saw in Toronto, which is sorely lacking in a place like Detroit.

Stewardship was originally made up of the tasks of a domestic steward, from stīġ (*house*, *hall*) and weard, (*ward*, *guard*, *guardian*, *keeper*). Stewardship, in the beginning, referred to the household servant's duties for bringing food and drink to the castle's dining hall. Stewardship responsibilities were eventually expanded to include everything of the domestic, service and management needs of the entire household. Stewardship is now generally recognized as the acceptance or assignment of *responsibility to shepherd and safeguard the valuables of others*.

One of Jesus' most well-known teachings is the Parable of the Talents (Matthew 25:14-30). Through this parable, Jesus tells us God's perspective on work, success, wealth, and especially about stewardship.

> *For it will be like a man going on a journey, who called his servants and entrusted to them his property. To one he gave five talents, to another two, to another one, to each according to his ability. Then he went away. He who had received the five talents went at once and traded with them, and he made five talents more. So also he who had the two*

talents made two talents more. But he who had received the one talent went and dug in the ground and hid his master's money. Now after a long time the master of those servants came and settled accounts with them. And he who had received the five talents came forward, bringing five talents more, saying, "Master, you delivered to me five talents; here I have made five talents more." His master said to him, "Well done, good and faithful servant. You have been faithful over a little; I will set you over much. Enter into the joy of your master." And he also who had the two talents came forward, saying, "Master, you delivered to me two talents; here I have made two talents more." His master said to him, "Well done, good and faithful servant. You have been faithful over a little; I will set you over much. Enter into the joy of your master." He also who had received the one talent came forward, saying, "Master, I knew you to be a hard man, reaping where you did not sow, and gathering where you scattered no seed, so I was afraid, and I went and hid your talent in the ground. Here you have what is yours." But his master answered him, "You wicked and slothful servant! You knew that I reap where I have not sown and gather where I scattered no seed? Then you ought to have invested my money with the bankers, and at my coming I should have received what was my own with interest. So take the talent from him and give it to him who has the ten talents. For to everyone who has will more be given, and he will have an abundance. But from the one who has not, even what he has will be taken away. And cast the worthless servant into the outer darkness. In that place there will be weeping and gnashing of teeth."

The Parable of the Talents offers a lot to contemplate. It also can be subject to different interpretations. Here are some of my thoughts about one of my favorite parables:

- **God does not micromanage us**. In the parable, the master gives the talents to his servants, and then he goes away. He doesn't give specific instructions of what to do with the talents; he expects them to utilize their own judgment on how to best utilize the resources at their disposal. The master is also gone for "a long time", probably several years. Even in Biblical times, doubling one's money without assuming excessive risk would take several years to accomplish.
- **We're not all created equal**. God may love us all equally, and we may all have equal rights under the law, but we're provided with a wide range of skills and abilities. The master recognizes this inequality by giving his first servant five times the responsibility of his third servant.
- **God focuses on our efforts, not our results**. Only God and parents recognize our efforts; the secular world recognizes only results. However, outcomes (results) are often beyond our control. Input (effort) is something we can control. Input has a direct bearing on outcome, though not always and not always in proportion. God recognizes this paradox and judges us by what is within our control.
- **God expects us to work**. While entry into Heaven is based on God's grace and not on a point system, God expects us to keep busy serving Him while we're here.

Those who think they have a punched ticket to Heaven because they proclaim Jesus as their savior, but then do nothing to further His kingdom on earth, may be in for a shock when their ticket is deemed invalid.

- **God likes an overachiever**. The master figured the first servant to be a superior steward to the second because he gave that servant two-and-a-half times the responsibility of the second. However, they both doubled the master's money during the same period of time. Since God does not miscalculate our natural abilities, the second servant must have worked harder than the first to achieve the same results. The master rewarded that overachievement by giving the same reward to both servants.
- **Blaming God for your failure is a major mistake**. The third servant mistakenly thought the best defense was a good offense. He accused the master of being a "hard man" and basically called him a parasite and a thief. The master would have none of it, pointing out that the servant could have done the minimum of putting the money with bankers to draw interest. Doing the minimum would not likely have earned any reward, but it would have at least avoided the punishment the "wicked and slothful" servant received.
- **God approves of honestly earned wealth**. The first two servants created wealth through hard work and diligence, which the master rewarded. The servants were also motivated by a desire to please the master, not by personal greed. Financial gain was not the cause, but the effect of doing the master's will.
- **God gives us everything we need to succeed**. Notice the third servant never claimed to lack the expertise to

grow the money entrusted to him. He and the master both knew he was capable; he just didn't bother to exercise his expertise for the benefit of the master. God knows our capabilities, which are usually far greater than what we think they are.

- **God gives us the opportunity to prove our love to him through stewardship**. Everyone, to varying degrees, has the opportunity every day to show God gratitude for the chance to serve Him. How well we act on those daily opportunities determines whether we'll enter into the joy of the master or be cast into the outer darkness.
- **God expects us to show initiative and take risks**. God doesn't just understand the positive correlation between risk and reward - He invented it. The third servant was so loss averse that he buried the master's money in the ground. The other two servants knew that some risk was necessary to grow wealth, and they proceeded accordingly. Success isn't possible without risking failure. God is OK with trying and failing; He's not OK with failing to try.
- **Jesus was preparing his disciples for his departure**. The master is typically interpreted as God, but in the parable, the master is gone for a long time, then returns. That part of the parable parallels with Jesus' return at some unknown time in the future. The servants are the disciples, and Jesus is reminding them of their duty to continue His work after He's gone.

In America, perhaps more than any society at any time in history, we bristle at the very terms "master" and "servant". We reject the notion that one person should be subservient to another, and our history of race relations makes us even more sensitive to the use of these terms.

Compulsory servitude should be rightly condemned. No one should be forced to serve another against their will. Our problem is, in our quest to eliminate masters, we feel compelled to eliminate servants, too. And when we eliminate servants, we eliminate service.

While they may not like terms like master and servant, people like to use the word "service" in describing what they do. A politician is in public *service.* A government worker is in civil *service.* A soldier is in military *service.* Veterans don't even specify military service; they simply say, "I was in the service." Because theirs is the highest form of service, they need say no more. We hold those who serve, which includes occupations such as teachers, nurses, and others where money is not the attraction, in high esteem. They serve because they want to, not because they're compelled by others or for financial gain, which is why they are (or should be) held in high esteem.

Stewardship is nothing but service to others and to God. You cannot be a good steward without being a good servant. Being a good servant means putting your ego aside and embracing something that's more important than you. That's not easy for humans in general and for Americans in particular, who learn early on that the individual is paramount.

When you enter the city limits of many cities and towns, next to the sign announcing the city you're entering is often another sign with various logos of groups that meet in that town. One of the logos you've seen is a wheel that looks like the toothed gear of a machine. It's the logo for Rotary International.

Rotary International is the largest service organization in the world, with over 34,000 clubs in more than 200 countries and more than 1.2 million total members; I'm one of them. Rotary was founded in 1905 by a Chicago attorney, Paul Harris. It began as a small group of business and professional people with diverse backgrounds who could exchange ideas and form meaningful, lifelong friendships. In a few years, the purpose expanded to provide humanitarian services, encourage high ethical standards in all vocations, and help build goodwill and peace in the world.

The motto of Rotary is "Service above Self". This motto is a perfect condensation of the entire concept of stewardship. It is, however, difficult to maintain such a high level of altruism day in and day out. Even the best of stewards has to occasionally ask of all their efforts, "What's in it for me?" Rotary has also provided the answer to that question in their previous motto, "One profits most who serves best."

Selflessness should be the defining characteristic of stewardship. However, we wouldn't be human or even survive for very long if we weren't mindful of our own self-interest (which is very different from selfishness). In the course of being a good steward, when you begin to wonder if you're working against your own self-interest, remember the first two servants in the Parable of the Talents. Nearly two-thousand years before Rotary, those servants understood that they profit most who serve best.

Stewardship is more than the giving of time, treasure, and talent. It's even more than taking care of the gifts God has given – spiritual, mental, physical, and material. Stewardship is first and foremost an attitude toward life.

Stewardship is about taking care of everything God has entrusted to you and being *thankful* for the opportunity to do so. It's not about giving for the sake of recognition or even appreciation.

There's nothing wrong per se in making a $10,000 donation to the church for the purchase of a new organ, with the proviso that a little plaque be attached to the organ recognizing your gift. However, I believe a truer example of stewardship is when you anonymously give $1,000 to the church to pay the electric bill. Giving money to specific causes within the church makes us feel good and important, but giving to the operating budget to pay for plumbers and pest control is done, not for recognition, but for the simple reason it *needs* to be done. The most important stewardship is often unseen. It's not unlike maintaining your car. People notice when you wash and wax your car; they don't notice when you change the oil. However, a shiny car is of little use if it won't run. And that beautiful organ won't make a sound if the electricity is shut off for non-payment.

The Cathedral Church of Saint Peter and Saint Paul in the City and Diocese of Washington D.C., operated under the more familiar name of Washington National Cathedral, is a cathedral of the Episcopal Church. Construction began on September 29, 1907 when President Theodore Roosevelt oversaw the laying of the foundation stone. Construction was completed in 1990, when President George H.W. Bush oversaw the installation of the "final finial". Even now, more than a century after construction began, decorative work is still being done on the sixth-largest cathedral in the world.

Like many of the great cathedrals and many more "small" churches, much of the work was done by volunteers who donated time and talent after working a full day at paying jobs. They also worked knowing full well they would never live to see the completed building. Most of us gather in a house of worship that others built. It would benefit us greatly to contemplate the sacrifice and stewardship of those who made our houses of worship possible. When it comes to places of worship, it's easier to maintain them than create them. We should demonstrate appreciation that we only have to maintain, not create, by being proper stewards of our places of worship.

Christians often give up something they enjoy for the forty days of Lent. Muslims refrain from eating, drinking, smoking, and sexual relations from sunrise to sunset during the month of Ramadan. The purpose of these sacrifices, like tithes and offerings, is to remind us that what we need most in life are not material things, but a deeper and more loving relationship with God.

When it comes to tithes and offerings, we tend to get the reasons for them all wrong. The purpose of giving money through tithes and offerings is *not* to raise money or pay for services. The fact that most offerings are used to support the religious organization makes it easy to conclude that the reason for giving is because the organization needs the money. The intent of tithes and offerings is spiritual and symbolic, not secular and economic. When done the right way and for the right reasons, stewardship and giving accrue more benefits to the giver than the receiver.

In Christian ethics, almsgiving has always been treated under the heading of justice rather than mercy. If we're all stewards and not owners, and if God's intent is to have the earth's resources used for the benefit of all, giving to meet the needs of the poor is simply giving them their fair share in the eyes of God.

Such notions can rub us the wrong way if we feel that we "earned" what we have while the poor did not. When we think like that, we're like the workers who worked all day in the parable of the workers in the vineyard (Matthew 20:1-16). The resources we think we own are not ours, and God's will is to make sure that all His children have enough. Stewardship begins by recognizing God's sovereignty over all.

Stewardship is about caring for God's gifts: spiritual, mental, physical, and material – in that order.

A gift is valued partly in relation to its rarity. Spiritual stewardship comes first because our spiritual nature is the most important gift from God, as evidenced by the fact that, among all God's creatures, only humans can begin to comprehend a higher being. We're first and foremost spiritual beings in a temporary human form; we're not human beings with occasional spiritual insights. Our first stewardship responsibility is to our spiritual stewardship because all else hinges on it.

Similar, but secondary to spiritual stewardship, is mental stewardship. I believe mental stewardship is second only to spiritual stewardship because we're unique creatures on the earth in our mental capacities as well.

Mental stewardship involves the continuous quest for both knowledge and wisdom. It recognizes that, as with our bodies, we need to constantly feed on what is healthy and to avoid what is unhealthy. Mental stewardship requires a constant expansion of our horizons. We should not only be learning new things, but learning new points of view as well. Mental stewardship also means giving our minds the chance to "Be still, and know that I am God." We need to take a mental Sabbath, if you will.

If data from various health studies are at all true, we have a lot of work to do regarding physical stewardship. Physical stewardship is important to prevent becoming a burden to others. More important, physical health, or rather the lack of it, can have an adverse effect on our ability to fulfill our stewardship duties in the spiritual, mental, and material realms. Physical stewardship is important, but we have to be careful not to carry it to the point of obsession and narcissism.

I've been a runner since 1969; I joined my high school cross-country team the week of Woodstock – the first one. I was a decent runner, though never outstanding, and I've recognized that, as a runner, I peaked sometime in the Nixon administration. However, even though I'm in my sixties and don't go as far or as fast as I used to, I recognize the importance of maintaining an exercise routine, which for me includes jogging three times a week. I even named my financial planning firm Marathon Financial Strategies. The name emphasizes that financial success takes persistence and discipline, as does running a marathon. Our tag line is "for the long run".

Whenever I would go for a run, my lovely wife Beth would tell me to "Enjoy!" I never gave it much thought until I began thinking about this book, and particularly this chapter. While a nice run on a pretty day when nothing is hurting is still enjoyable, enjoyment is not my reason for running. In fact, running is one way I'm reminded I'm no longer young. Even if I work harder, I'll still only be slower than I was in my youth. Running makes me grateful I can still do it, but pounding pavement and sucking wind for forty-five minutes at a stretch is almost never an enjoyable experience. Since my wife's comment led me to this contemplation of why

I run, she no longer tells me to enjoy. Now it's more like, "Don't hurt yourself."

My running has almost nothing to do with enjoyment. It has almost everything to do with stewardship. Like you, I've been granted one body to last a lifetime. The actual quality and quantity of that lifetime is directly related to how well I take care of this body. Running is one of the many things I do to increase both the quality and quantity of my life.

When I was a runner in high school, I remember an old man sitting on his front porch as I ran by telling me that he didn't run because he only had so many heartbeats; therefore, he didn't want to waste any of them like I was doing. His comment sent my mental calculator whirring.

The average person has a resting pulse rate of 72 bpm (beats per minute). Mine is about 60 bpm, and has been since 1969. Even after allowing for the extra beats of exercise, my heart beats about 90,000 fewer times in a week than it would if I didn't exercise and had a normal rate of 72 bpm. If that old man were right, and if we each have a predetermined number of heartbeats, the 90,000 heartbeats I save every week adds more than a day to my life - every single week.

The process of exercise may not always be pleasant (though it doesn't have to be *un*pleasant), but the increase in both the quality and quantity of life makes it worth the effort. But even if exercise didn't improve my chances of longevity, it would be valuable as preventive maintenance. If you think the cost of repairs are expensive on your car, it's nothing compared to repairing the human body. Ben Franklin's advice that an ounce of prevention is worth a pound of cure has stewardship written all over it.

I have one big advantage in my exercise routine – habit. The physical effort expended is fairly constant; if it diminished, so would the value of the exercise. The mental effort expended to exercise is next to nothing. After decades of doing it, the habit is so ingrained that it takes a mental effort *not* to exercise regularly. My exercise routine is simply stewardship made easier through *habit*.

If you were to categorize people on a sliding scale, based on the quality of their stewardship, and you then categorized the same people on the number and strength of their good and bad habits, you would likely see a strong correlation. People with good habits tend to be good stewards; people with bad habits tend to be bad stewards.

The cause and effect pattern may go both ways. People with a natural tendency to be good stewards are conscientious by nature. A conscientious person is more likely to develop good habits and avoid bad ones.

Some habits matter more than others. Such habits are ones that, when they change, other habits change as well. These are known as *keystone habits*, and changing one of these for the better can have ripple effects in many other areas.

Exercise is considered a keystone habit. Once people begin an exercise habit, they reconsider other habits that are likely to undo the progress made by exercise. A positive change in a keystone habit pays unforeseen benefits in areas that might seem to be unrelated. The development of keystone habits creates wider changes in behavior, among them an improvement in a person's level of conscientiousness and of stewardship.

Material stewardship involves maintaining our possessions, but it goes deeper than that. Material stewardship also recognizes that material things come after the spiritual, the mental, and the physical. Time, money, and effort expended on material stewardship that come at the expense of necessary spiritual, mental, or physical stewardship can be considered a step backward in one's total stewardship progress. It's for this reason that keeping one's material possessions to a minimum is important to overall stewardship. With every possession comes a duty of care. We already have a soul, a mind, and a body, and caring for them is a full-time job. While we must take care of those possessions we *need*, limiting the possessions we merely *want* will greatly improve our chances of devoting our stewardship energies where they're most needed.

A true stewardship mentality requires a major shift in the way those of us in a materialistic culture think. From a secular perspective, the question is, "What do I need to give?" From the spiritual perspective, the question is, "What do I have a right to keep?" In a country like the United States, where property rights are perhaps our most protected rights, believing we don't have the right to keep everything that comes into our possession requires some serious mental adjustments.

Among the many confusions humans have regarding money and property, one of the biggest involves *ownership* and *possession*. Specifically, we sacrifice for ownership when possession is what we really want.

Like many families, my family enjoys taking vacations to places like the mountains or the beach. When we get there and settle in, we'll often sit and look out over the mountains or the water and a thought will cross my mind – Wouldn't it be nice to *own* a place like this? Fortunately, I'm able to suppress the siren song of these vistas by remembering that I already *possess* the place, which is what I really want.

I've known many people who go to a favorite vacation spot and end up buying a second home, condo, or time share there. They love it so much they just *have to own it!* What they fail to realize when they're under love's spell is they're trading the advantages of possession for the disadvantages of ownership.

When you own a vacation home, it actually owns you more than you own it. First, it owns your time. Because you've spent a large sum of money to obtain ownership, you now feel obligated to justify that expense by spending as much time there as possible. You may enjoy spending time there, but you sacrifice the option of going other places and having new experiences whenever you go instead to your vacation home.

The vacation home owns the time you're there in another way. Often, you may spend some of that time attending to the maintenance of the property. Even if you do no maintenance of the property yourself, you almost certainly have to pay someone for certain maintenance services. The money to pay for those services comes from time you sacrifice working to get it. Either way, the maintenance of a vacation home exacts a toll in time from its owner.

Whatever the price of the vacation home, there is an *opportunity cost* to own it. Every dollar spent on a mortgage payment, condo fee, tax bill, or maintenance contract is a dollar that doesn't have the opportunity to benefit you by some other use. And considering the cost of owning and maintaining most vacation homes, that's a lot of opportunity cost.

When our vacation time is up, I'm able to turn in the keys and walk away. I've enjoyed unrestricted possession of the property, with none of the obligations of ownership. I didn't have to waste a minute of precious vacation time worrying about the property. I'm free to go wherever I want on my next vacation, including a return to the same place. And all I take back with me are pleasant memories.

It's important to have legal ownership of the things we truly *need*, but ownership of things we merely *want* is a trap that requires a level of sacrifice we rarely realize until it becomes unbearable. Ownership makes demands and exacts a financial penalty if those demands aren't met.

The whole concept of stewardship is based on the principle that we don't really own anything. Everything is owned by God, and God lets us have possession as long as we take care. God lets us play with His toys, but we're supposed to be careful with them. This concept is nothing new – we all had such experiences as children when we got the chance to play with someone else's toys, though we had to be careful not to break anything.

While the Scriptures acknowledge the material world, they have no sympathy with materialism. Hedonism, narcissism, and materialism, which tend to travel together, are all severely judged.

Humans were created by God to be the caretakers, the trustees, the stewards of the earth. The earth and its resources are the corpus of a trust created by God the grantor, and we are the trustees.

In a trust, the corpus refers to the assets in the trust that are not to be touched. Those assets can be used to generate income for the beneficiaries (that would be us, too), but not at the expense of endangering or reducing the corpus of the trust. When well-managed, the corpus should grow over time, even while generating income.

The care and growth of the corpus enables benefits to increase while enabling the trust to continue indefinitely.

Like trusts created by humans, this trust between God and humans allows the grantor to void the trust and reclaim ownership of the corpus if the trustees fail to perform their duties to an acceptable level. Our duty is to *use* God's gifts to benefit mankind now, and to *protect* God's gifts to benefit mankind in the future.

In this world, we have *social norms* and *market norms*. Social norms involve the interactions between humans. They're about helping each other and getting along. They're the glue that holds a society together. They're biological. Market norms involve a bottom line. They're transaction-based. They can be precisely measured. They're mechanical.

Stewardship has everything to do with social norms and nothing to do with market norms.

The first thing to realize is that when social norms collide with market norms, social norms lose. This collision almost always occurs when market norms invade the world of social norms. In the case of stewardship, when someone creates an if-then proposition (i.e. - "I'll give you $100,000 for the new Christian Ed. Building if you name it after me."), they take what should have been an act of stewardship and generosity in the arena of social norms and turned it into a business negotiation thoroughly controlled by market norms.

In social relationships, social norms should rule. When you're invited to a friend's house for dinner, you bring a nice bottle of wine as a gift; you don't offer to "pay the tab" at the end of the evening. When your neighbor asks to borrow your lawn mower, you lend it with the expectation he will reciprocate and return the favor in the future; you don't charge him rent. When your community of faith reaches out to you, either for help or to help, your response should be gratitude for the help or for the ability to help.

Social norms should always prevail when a higher calling is involved, which certainly includes anything spiritual. People are more inclined to donate blood when cookies and juice are offered as a thank you than when cash is offered as compensation. If people want to do something for altruistic reasons, you offend them and prompt them to withdraw support if you bring money into the equation. The good feeling we get when we do something to help others is priceless, so the worst thing one can do is attempt to put a price on it.

One of the best examples of social norms, market norms, and reciprocity is in *The Godfather*. The opening scene has Bonasera, the undertaker, asking Don Corleone to kill the men who violated his daughter. The Don replies, "What have I done to make you treat me so disrespectfully? You don't ask this favor out of friendship. Instead you come to my house on the day of my daughter's wedding and ask me to do murder for money." Don Corleone refuses to let market norms trump social norms. While I would never intimate that the Godfather is actually a Godlike figure, we often act like Bonasera when we try to negotiate with God using market norms. We don't have anything God wants except our love, respect, and obedience to Him. It's to be offered as our gift to God with no strings attached.

If you introduce market norms where social norms prevail, market norms will almost always win. But know that social norms may never return and that they never forget, either.

Our social network, our relationship support system, is undergirded by social norms. When we're clumsy with social norms or when we attempt to replace social norms with market norms, we risk knocking that entire support system out from under us. Poor use of social norms can even turn friends into enemies.

The following is a breakdown of average household expenditures by percentage of household income in 1973 and in 2013, forty years later:

Category	1973	2013
Food	17.4%	12.8%
Housing	27.8%	32.8%
Household Supplies/Operation	4.1%	3.5%
Electricity/Gas	3.4%	3.7%
Telephone	2.0%	2.4%
Transportation	16.5%	17.5%
Healthcare	5.8%	6.9%
Savings	10.1%	4.6%
401k/Social Security	3.7%	6.1%
Church/Charity	5.7%	3.7%
Uncategorized/Discretionary	3.5%	6.0%

Further analysis of these figures reveals the following:

- In 1973, the average new home was 1,525 square feet; in 2013 it was 2,679 square feet. In 1973, the average household had 3.01 occupants; in 2013 it had 2.54 occupants. In 1973, there was 507 square feet per occupant; by 2013, that figure had more than doubled to 1,055 square feet.
- Food costs have dropped due to more efficient production methods. Average caloric consumption has risen slightly, mostly due to a tripling of the calories we consume outside the home in restaurants. The increase in obesity is driven primarily by poor stewardship of our bodies. In the last twenty years

alone, the percentage of women who have no physical activity has nearly tripled; the percentage of men has quadrupled.

- Transportation spending has risen slightly, though cars are far more reliable and better-equipped than their 1973 counterparts. Most of the standard features on the most basic family car weren't even available in 1973, and those that were, such as air-conditioning, were very expensive compared to today.
- Very few people have employer funded retirement plans compared to 1973, yet retirement funding and savings have dropped from 13.8% to 10.7%. We should be saving more than in 1973 to make up for the decline in employer funding, but we're saving less, even though the need to save is greater than in 1973.
- Most alarmingly, charitable giving (which includes funding of religious organizations) has dropped by more than one-third in the last forty years as a percentage of household income.

We've reduced our charitable giving to buy bigger homes. When we doubled our square footage per person, we also doubled our average home size compared to the average of all other developed countries. These larger homes also have more amenities than their foreign and 1973 counterparts.

Our cars aren't bigger than in 1973, but they are more reliable, safer, more efficient, and far more comfortable than those of forty years ago. A five-year-old car today is superior in every way to a brand new car of forty years ago. It's no longer necessary to have a new car to have reliable, safe, comfortable transportation.

Stewardship is about action, not words; talking about stewardship is worthless without the actions to back up the talk. How we spend our money says more about our priorities than anything else we do or say.

We can give our talent freely because our talent does not diminish with use; it actually increases. We also enjoy the ego boost we get from showing off our talents. We can give time more freely than money because we don't see it as finite as money. The preciseness and finiteness of money, however, makes it very clear to us what we are giving away when we give away money. That exactness makes it that much harder to let go.

If you want to see what kind of steward you are, one of the best places to start is with your checkbook. You can create a list like the one above and categorize all your monthly expenses. It's best to track your spending for several months to get an accurate indication of your spending patterns over time. I recommend you start with gross income and include categories for money withheld from your paycheck, such as health insurance and taxes.

After a few months of tracking spending, see how your percentages compare to the average American family. If your income is considerably higher or lower than average, your percentages will probably vary to a greater degree from the average.

More important, see how your percentages compare to what you thought you were spending, and also to what you want to be spending in each category. If you're like many (most?) people, you may be surprised how little you actually give to charity as a percentage of income. You may also feel a twinge of embarrassment at how charitable giving is sacrificed for other category spending, like a bigger home or a nicer car.

People become very private about money when it comes to their levels of debt and their levels of giving. The desire for privacy is not surprising when the disclosure could prove embarrassing. If, after accumulating your spending data over the next six months, you then had to post it on Facebook, Twitter, or other social media for all your friends to see, how would you feel about it? If the mere thought of such disclosure makes you uncomfortable, it may be time to reevaluate your personal financial stewardship program, or to implement one if you don't already have one.

In the course of my writing, I've had the opportunity to give serious consideration to what my mission is in life. In another of my books, *Becoming Whealthy*, I discuss the importance of discovering one's own mission. In order to advise others on their missions, I had to first clarify my own. I came up with these:

- Conduct myself in a manner that brings honor to my God, my family, my community, and my profession.
- Be a proper steward of all that has been entrusted to me, both material and non-material.
- Use my knowledge and experience as a financial professional to help others become more financially secure.
- Serve as a role model for my clients and any others who may look to me for inspiration and guidance.
- Do everything possible to prevent becoming a burden to my family, my friends, or my community.
- Don't merely leave the woodpile higher than I found it, but add as much to it as possible during my lifetime.

It didn't occur to me when I was articulating my missions how much stewardship played a role. The last three missions require active stewardship. I wouldn't be a very good role model for anyone if I didn't act as a proper steward of everything I possess or control. Who's going to follow the financial advice of someone whose own financial house is in disarray? How can I encourage a healthy lifestyle to others if my behaviors jeopardize my own health?

I loathe the idea of becoming dependent on others, and I especially loathe the idea of becoming dependent because I didn't take care of myself physically, mentally, financially, or spiritually. Circumstances beyond my control may require my dependence on others in the future, but in the meantime I plan to do all I can to prevent that dependence from happening.

Paul Harvey offered many words of wisdom over six decades in broadcasting. As a fourteen-year-old listener in 1968, but I'll always remember his challenge to "Leave the woodpile higher than you found it." I love the woodpile metaphor for several reasons. For millennia, wood was the primary source of fuel. It was essential for heating, cooking, and light. It was as essential to survival as food and water for many people. It was so essential, there were community woodpiles to make sure everyone had enough wood to at least keep from freezing to death. The woodpile was regulated, and citizens were expected to not exploit this public asset, and to add to it as their circumstances enabled them.

The community woodpile and our responsibility to leave it higher than we found it is the essence of stewardship. No one owns the woodpile, yet we all have a responsibility to it. The benefits of maintaining the woodpile accrue to everyone, including those people who maintain it. Those who don't do their part to maintain will eventually suffer, but so will those who do more than their part. Short-term self-interest is why you take from the woodpile; long-term self-interest is why you give to the woodpile. No one wants to be labeled a parasite and ostracized from the community, nor is it in anyone's interest to see the community woodpile concept abandoned because the community as a whole took more than it gave.

While the notion of the community woodpile and the call to leave it higher than you found it are noble, human nature works against it. When everybody owns something, such as the woodpile, no one owns it; consequently, no one feels they have a direct interest in maintaining or improving its condition. While we may admire the notion of "One for all and all for one", we're more likely to act on the notion of "Every man for himself."

"Every man for himself" is the antithesis of "Service above Self" and is the antithesis of stewardship as well. True stewardship requires us to swim against the current of our human nature. But going against the current of human nature is how we move closer to God.

THE SWEAT OF YOUR BROW AND YOUR BRAIN

Question: Who is responsible for the Beatles, night baseball, *The Godfather*, and the "crawler" at the bottom of the screen on CNN? Answer: Thomas Edison (seen above with his phonograph).

Four of Edison's most well-known inventions are the phonograph, the electric light, the movie projector, and the stock ticker. Without those inventions, the above list doesn't happen.

Perhaps more than anyone else in history, Thomas Edison seems the perfect fit for the work he did. He held 1,093 patents on his inventions. He had so many things going on at once, he had to start a company to keep everything running smoothly. We know it as General Electric.

Thomas Edison was known for his work habits. Twenty-hour workdays and hundred-hour workweeks were common. I've estimated that Edison worked over 14,000,000 minutes in his life. (12 hour days; 6 day weeks; 50 weeks/year; 65 years).

Edison famously said, "Genius is 1% inspiration, and

99% perspiration." He recognized the sweat of the brain and the brow were necessary for success.

How could someone work like that for more than sixty years without burning out? Edison loved his work so much he didn't *want* to do anything else. Edison spent the better part of two years creating a practical light bulb. He tested thousands of filaments (over six thousand plant filaments alone) before finding one that would last. It may seem obsessive-compulsive to most of us, but look at the results. Turn on a light first; you'll see better.

Edison is the poster boy for what kind of success is possible when the right person is in the right job. Edison points out in his biography that it isn't hard work that kills someone (He died at 84.), it's stress and worry. Few things are more worrisome than wondering if you're wasting your life doing the wrong work.

I've estimated that the average person will spend some 6,000,000 minutes of their life on their work. Let's start at age 18, right after high school. Even if a person goes on to college, the main purpose of getting a college degree is to improve career choices, so I consider college to be time invested at work. If the average workday is 8 hours and if the average daily commute is 30 minutes (Your commute counts toward work time.), that's 510 minutes per day. If the average person works 240 days per year, that's 2,040 hours, or 122,400 minutes per year of work. If retirement comes at 67 (the youngest age for full social security benefits), the total minutes worked comes to 5,997,600. A mere 44 hours of overtime over a 49-year work period will bring the total to over 6,000,000 minutes.

There are countless ways that people define work. Most of them involve an exchange of time and talent for treasure. For the moment, I want to exclude money from the following definition: work is doing what you *have* to do; play is doing what you *want* to do.

If work is defined as doing what you have to do, then many of the things we have to do qualify as work, even though we don't get paid to do them. On the other hand, if we get paid for doing things we want to do, it's like getting paid to play. Given the choice, I would rather be like Edison and spend 14,000,000 minutes of my life getting paid to do things I want to do, than spend 6,000,000 minutes (or even 6,000,000 seconds) doing things I have to do, even if I'm getting paid for it.

Edison invented many things, but his first and most important invention was his career. Then as now, there were no colleges where one could learn to become an inventor. Edison learned at an early age what he was good at and what he loved to do. One of the reasons he loved what he did was he could see the benefits to mankind that his work produced. He invented a career that enabled him to do what he did best, and that career gave people many ways to make their lives better.

People who are doing work that's ill-suited for them are easy to spot – they look like a square peg in a round hole. It's certainly no fun feeling like that square peg, getting pounded into that round hole day after day. Let's also remember it's no fun for the hole, either. When someone is in the wrong job, the employee, the employer, and the customers all suffer. It's a lose-lose-lose proposition.

For better or worse, much of our identity is connected to our work. When you meet someone for the first time, one of the first questions people ask is, "What do you do for a living?" Many of us strive to have an impressive answer to that question, even if the most correct answer might be, "I'm a square peg in a round hole." If your career choice were based largely on impressing others or making money (often the same thing), then the pain of being a square peg in a round hole is on you.

Many people believe that happiness from work is the result of being successful at work. The opposite is in fact true. Success at work is the result of being happy at work. Going back to the square-peg-round-hole analogy, believing that success leads to happiness at work is like believing that everything will be just fine if that square peg will just get into that round hole. Even if the square peg makes it, it's not going to be happy. On the other hand, a square peg in a square hole is a natural fit and is naturally happy. In that environment, the square peg can happily fulfill its mission.

Think about some of your own life circumstances. Did you ever work at something that you didn't particularly like and weren't particularly good at doing? Did you make yourself continue, with the expectation that achieving success would bring with it happiness? And did you find that the happiness you experienced upon achieving success was less than you expected, or worse, that happiness never materialized at all?

Did you ever work at something for which you had a love and a passion, as well as a talent? Even if you weren't naturally talented, did you find working to improve your talent didn't feel like work because you enjoyed everything about it, even the drudgery? Did you find that failures along the way didn't discourage you, but provided valuable opportunities to learn and become better? And did success eventually come, and did success seem inevitable, even during the most challenging periods?

If you've had either of those experiences, and especially if you've had both, then you know from personal experience that happiness doesn't follow success; success follows happiness, at least where our work is concerned.

It's a waste and a tragedy that so few people manage to find work that makes them happy. When it does happen, it's often by accident, as opposed to a conscious effort to seek out the right fit for our talents and passions. For too many, their career path is nothing more than an assemblage of the best-paying jobs that crossed their paths.

There's nothing wrong with taking a position that pays more, everything else being equal. However, the one area where jobs are almost never equal is the happiness and fulfillment one gets from the job. Because we can't easily quantify happiness like we can salary, happiness often becomes subordinated to salary in our career decisions. This subordination to money will often end up resulting in less happiness and less money.

Recall that success does not lead to happiness; happiness leads to success. Our pay level at work is almost always directly correlated with how successful we are at performing the duties of our job. If happiness leads to greater success and if greater success leads to greater incomes, it's only logical that seeking work that leads to greater happiness will inevitably lead to greater income, if not immediately, then soon thereafter.

The paradox of work is then this – the way to make the most money from your work is to not think about money, but focus instead on work that will make you happy. Happiness in doing something often occurs initially because we have some natural ability in that area. That high starting point makes the hard work of honing those skills less tedious and more rewarding. The happiness that comes from doing the work itself, combined with the head start of any natural ability, creates a work ethic that leads to greater success, which leads to greater financial rewards.

Unfortunately, traditional career counseling doesn't work that way. Young people are urged into hot job sectors for the money and the (hypothetical) job security. And since so many college students assume large debts to obtain a degree, short-term financial rewards have a disproportionate influence on their decisions. Our traditional education system focuses on *how* someone should do certain kinds of work without ever asking *why* someone should be doing that kind of work.

Before people can know what kind of work will make them happy, they need to know something about themselves. Among other things, they need to know how they gather and process information, how they make decisions, how they relate to the outside world, how they start, implement, and follow through on projects, and even what their character strengths and weaknesses are.

There are all kinds of evaluation methods to help someone determine what might be a good career path. Here are four resources that could prove useful:

- **Myers-Briggs Type Indicator**: a psychometric questionnaire designed to measure psychological preferences in how people perceive the world and make decisions. It's an expansion of Carl Jung's work in the 1920s and is sometimes called the Jung Typology Test. The MBTI measures four criteria, leading to one of sixteen personality types. It can be taken at www.humanmetrics.com.

- **Keirsey Temperament Sorter**: In the same vein as MBTI/Jung, this "personality instrument" classifies people into one of four temperaments – artisan, guardian, rational, or idealist. KTS-II, as it's called, can help clarify and reinforce results from the MBTI. It can be taken at www.keirsey.com.
- **Kolbe A Index/Instinct Test**: While personality tests like MBTI and Keirsey can tell you what you want to do, the Kolbe test is designed to tell you what you will or won't do. It evaluates methods of operation based on natural instincts. This test enables the right person, the right project, and the right team to match up. It can be taken at www.kolbe.com.
- **Character Strengths Test:** Among several tests developed by two psychologists at the University of Pennsylvania, this test measures your level of 24 character strengths, such as persistence, fairness, creativity, and spirituality. They also have several tests that measure happiness and work-life satisfaction. They can be taken at www.authentichappiness.org.

You're probably familiar with some version of the 80/20 principle. In churches, the 80/20 principle manifests itself whereby 20% of the congregation gives 80% of the money and does 80% of the work.

Another application of the 80/20 principle is in our work. In most of our undertakings, including work, 80% of our results come from 20% of our efforts. If you think about the times you've been really productive, on a hot streak, in *flow*, you were accomplishing a lot with relatively little effort. In those situations, you felt great, and it was easy to love your work. The other 80% of the time – well, that's another story.

One of the benefits of taking the kinds of evaluations listed above is finding out the 20% that will yield 80%. Some people may see taking such evaluations as a waste of time, but nothing is more wasteful than dedicating 80% of your time and effort for a yield of 20%. That's an outcome/input ratio of 1:4. I would certainly find the time to learn how I can reverse that outcome/input ratio from 1:4 to 4:1.

As an example, take the character strengths test. There are 24 character strengths measured in this test. Your top 5 character strengths are the 20% that yield 80% of your results. It's important to know what those strengths are so you can fully utilize them to achieve your goals.

You'll also find out your greatest character weaknesses. We all have some, and I don't recommend making the huge investment of time and effort to turn those weaknesses into strengths; it would be extremely unproductive. However, by becoming aware of your greatest weaknesses, you can minimize the damage they might cause you. The weaknesses will likely never help you move forward; your goal is to keep them from moving you backward.

Evaluations like these can help you understand what kind of work you should be doing, who you should be doing it with, and how you should be doing it. They can even offer some insight into the most important question – *why* you want to and should be doing a particular kind of work.

If the answer to the question of why you're doing a particular kind of work is that it pays the most, that's evidence that the cause and effect relationship with money is backwards. Money is the effect of our work; it's not the cause of it.

If the only reason you can give for the work you do is the paycheck you get, you're shortchanging yourself on one of the most important benefits of work – the joy of contribution. If all it would take for you to change jobs is a modest raise, it's time to find work that provides more than a paycheck, even if it's a decent paycheck.

Anyone who's ever taken a psychology course is familiar with *Maslow's Hierarchy of Needs*. Abraham Maslow developed his theory in 1943. The hierarchy is, in descending order:

- **Self-Actualization** (morality, creativity, spontaneity)
- **Esteem** (achievement, confidence, respect from others)
- **Love/Belonging** (friendship, family, sexual intimacy)
- **Safety** (physical security, employment, health, family)
- **Physiological** (breathing, food, water, sleep, sex)

Maslow theorized that, until one's needs are met at the lower levels, one cannot or will not devote energy to meeting needs at the higher levels. This assumption is valid - you can't focus on your job if you haven't had enough sleep or food; you can't focus on friendships if you're about to lose your job; you can't focus on becoming a more well-rounded person when a loved one is battling a life-threatening disease. The hierarchy of needs is one way of measuring how well we're achieving our full potential.

There's a similar hierarchy when we look at our work. If you're out of work, it can become a desperate struggle just to meet the physiological needs at the bottom of the hierarchy. When you do get a job, you hope it will pay enough to meet your physiological needs. You seek to stay with an employer and hopefully get some raises and promotions in order to fulfill your safety needs. However, when a job is just a job, it won't provide much more than these basic needs. Because these jobs neither demand much nor provide much, you may put your back into it, but not your heart and soul.

Most people aspire to have more than a job - they want a career. A career is a series of jobs that enables you to move up on the hierarchy of needs. A career will usually enable you to buy more of the things that people seek on the lower level of needs. The most attractive aspect of a career is that it offers the opportunity to fulfill some esteem needs. If we didn't consider esteem to be so highly valued, people wouldn't work to earn a Ph.D. in English Literature for the opportunity to teach a core class at the local community college. They would go instead to a two-year trade school and learn plumbing, where they could then go out and charge $75 an hour for their services.

If you're lucky, a job leads to a career. If you're luckier, your career becomes your vocation. A vocation is defined as an occupation or profession for which a person is especially suited or qualified. Someone who merely works in a job may be a square peg in a round hole. Someone who builds a career is likely to be a square peg in a square hole, though more careers are made by reshaping a round peg into a square one than by reshaping a square hole into a round one. With a vocation, you're not only a square peg in a square hole; you're the right size peg for that hole.

Finally, we have the pinnacle of the work hierarchy, the *calling*. We often think of callings in terms of religions, but a calling can be any work that benefits others primarily and the worker secondarily. A calling is just that – you feel that this is the work God put you on this earth to do. You've been called *by God* to do it. A calling is your ministry, even if the work you do is of a secular nature and if you're paid well to do it. Ministry and money don't have to be mutually exclusive.

When you merely have a job, you do the job for the pay. If there's any non-monetary benefit to the job, it won't keep you from leaving for a modest raise elsewhere. With a career, there are benefits beyond pay, but you're unlikely to change careers if you couldn't make as much money in the new career, even if you enjoyed the work more.

When you have a vocation, you continuously find it hard to believe that you actually get paid to do something you love. You're not about to give up the financial benefits, but they assume secondary importance to what you receive beyond the paycheck. Finally, a calling is work that you would pay money to others for the privilege of performing. You're so drawn to do that work and you're so called by that work that it doesn't matter what you have to do in order to work in that field – you'll do it. With a vocation, a person usually starts out with a skill set that makes that vocation a rewarding and easy choice. With a calling, a skill set may have to be acquired through years of training, and even then it might not be enough.

When viewed through the prism of Maslow's Hierarchy of Needs, most jobs take a bottom-up approach. The job promises to provide money in exchange for work, and that money can be used to supply one's basic needs. The reason most people can't get passionate about their jobs is that the job doesn't provide an opportunity to release their passions. Without passion for your work, the most you're likely to become in that work is "competent", which means you are capable of competing (but not necessarily winning).

A calling takes a top-down approach regarding the hierarchy of needs. A calling speaks to something inside the individual that promises to make him or her a better person, typically by providing the opportunity for that person to make the world a better place. A calling will provide you with the needs at the top of the hierarchy first, especially self-actualization. Our more basic needs get met as our passion for our work leads to becoming more than competent in performing it. By excellently providing something of value to people, those being served then provide the means to meet all the servant's more basic needs.

The lower levels of the hierarchy of needs focus on feeding the purse alone. They often do so at the expense of the body, mind, and soul. At most, one can hope the soul isn't being harmed by one's work, which is not to say there's no value to work that provides only a paycheck. If a certain kind of work didn't provide something of value to others, people wouldn't pay for it.

It may be possible to transform your current job into your calling, but it's a tough job working from the bottom up to make such a change. I also don't recommend you quit your job, pitch a tent in the woods, and contemplate your true calling for the next year. I recommend you first look at your current situation and see if there's the potential to transform your job into a calling, to be pulled rather than pushed into getting up each day and going to work. In the meantime, do some soul-searching to ask yourself what kind of work you could do that:

a) would give you a sense of purpose;
b) would be within your capabilities at some point;
c) would enable you to meet your more basic needs as well.

It might take years to find your true calling, but the first step in finding your true calling is to realize you have one and to begin looking for it.

When assessing where your work puts you on Maslow's Hierarchy of Needs, ask yourself, "Am I a missionary or a mercenary?" Missionaries are at the top; mercenaries are at the bottom. Where are you?

People are inspired to greatness; they're almost never motivated to it. Inspiration draws you; motivation shoves you. It's just too exhausting to be shoved all the way to greatness. If you're merely motivated by family, friends, peers, greed, fear, competitors, enemies, or a thousand other "motivating factors," you may achieve greatness, but it will feel empty and, more importantly, it will be fleeting. Greatness built on motivation without inspiration is like a foundation that's made with concrete that has too much sand and not enough cement. It may look solid, but time quickly exposes the weakness, and whatever was built on that foundation soon collapses.

The goal is to become inspired in your work or to find inspiring work. Your work can be whatever you define it to be; it doesn't have to be something you do for pay, although almost everything we do for pay is classified as work. For most of us, work is the primary, if not the sole, source of income. Work occupies more waking hours than any other single activity for almost everyone who works full-time.

Regardless of whether you become a doctor, a business owner, or a fry cook at McDonalds, your success will ultimately be measured by how those you serve perceive the quality of your work. Talent, degrees, and even celebrity will not protect you from the judgment of those people. The best businesses recognize that shareholder satisfaction and employee satisfaction are the direct result of customer satisfaction.

Many people work in jobs where they don't have direct contact with customers; that's irrelevant. The assembly line worker is far from the customer, but if the quality of that person's work is substandard, it will show up in the product. Customer complaints and lost sales will be noticed by management, who will seek out the source of the problem. They'll find it soon enough, and if the worker is at fault, that worker will soon be out of work.

Everyone who ever uttered the phrase, "It's not my job" has probably done more harm to their careers than they realize. Those words can be like fingernails on a blackboard to an employer, and they never forget those who utter them.

Part of the blame for such an employee attitude can be placed on the job description. Employers create job descriptions so employees can be held accountable for performing the duties listed in that job description. The implication, though, is that the stated duties are the only duties for which the employee is responsible. When an employer sets a floor of expectations regarding what an employee is to do, they unknowingly also set a ceiling on what they could expect an employee to do. Unions will codify this ceiling into labor contracts, which don't merely discourage, but may expressly forbid an employee doing work outside of specified duties.

Job duties that are too specific can have the unintended consequence of stifling initiative. Initiative is to an enterprise as hormones are to the body. Initiative is more abundant in smaller, newer enterprises because there are many things to be done and too few people to do them. Saying, "It's not my job." in these organizations doesn't work because everyone is doing everything that needs to be done to make the business successful. When organizations become large and bureaucratic, job duties get more specific; every task is expected to be assigned in a job description, and employees are less likely to show initiative by performing additional duties.

Every organization needs to make sure they have a culture in place that encourages employees to make suggestions, to offer improvements, to improve efficiencies and customer service without fear they might be criticized for overstepping their responsibilities. Employees, for their part, need to look for ways to do all of the above, even if management isn't initially receptive. Any organization that stifles employee initiative is not a place that any employee with initiative should want to remain. The employee is better off using that initiative to find a workplace where its use is encouraged and rewarded.

If people truly believe in the mission of the organization that employs them, they should want to do everything within their power to help that organization accomplish that mission. If that means doing work that falls outside the normal day-to-day duties of their job, they should be willing to do so. Of course, no employer should ask any employee to do anything that violates an individual's ethics or the law. Employees should also know the difference between a good employer who is asking everyone for their best effort and an employer who exploits and abuses the employees.

Research has shown that it typically takes only a 5% raise to compel an unhappy employee to change employers, but it takes at least a 20% raise to compel a happy employee to change. When people are happy in their work environment, their preference is to stay rather than take a risk by changing jobs. When workers aren't happy, they'll assume that almost anyplace is better than where they are now, so it takes very little financial incentive to get them to move.

When people talk about bosses they held in high regard, a common description of them is "firm but fair." If a boss isn't firm, the slackers will slack, and the good workers will have to pick up that slack. If they aren't fair, anyone who isn't getting favored treatment is resentful.

The firm-but-fair boss is able to balance the concern for results (firm) and the concern for people (fair). It's more art than science, which is why truly great bosses can be rare. Great bosses can still be unappreciated by some workers. Those workers often end up losing their jobs and realize how good they had it only after they discover the flaws in their new boss.

To be firm but fair requires constant reassessing and recalibration. Both the needs of the employees and the needs of the organization are constantly changing. In tough economic times, it can be easy to assume that less attention should be given to the employees to focus more attention on the health of the organization.

The attention a boss gives to the organization and the employees is not a fixed total, though. Greater attention to one should not come at the expense of the other. In fact, during tough economic times, a good boss ramps up attention to both the organization and the employees, who feel vulnerable during this period and need to know the boss has them covered. Great bosses are actually made during the tough times because they have to carry extra-heavy loads of firmness and fairness, while keeping them both balanced.

When we were in school, the one adjective we hoped

would be ascribed to us was *popular*. There was often recognition of the most popular students at the prom or in the yearbook. Then something happened during the transition from school to work. Evaluations of popularity ceased. Instead of being lauded for being popular, we now had a new accolade to strive for - *competent*.

In the workplace, the only person who might be classified as popular is likely a perky-but-competent low-level employee who isn't considered a threat to anyone. The popular person in the office may be universally liked, but no one aspires to be that person, at least not within the work environment.

In the workplace, the only thing that matters are results. Results are measurable, while effort is not. Results are also comparable, and the world uses them to see how you compare to your competition. The world is a very bottom-line place, and effort that doesn't translate into results doesn't help the bottom line. When your parents said that life isn't fair, this is one reality to which they were referring.

Profit isn't about taking advantage of workers, which will cause a company to soon fail. Profit isn't about enriching shareholders, although shareholders are entitled to a reward commensurate with their risk. Profit is about supplying the company with the lifeblood to keep going.

Without profit, a company cannot adapt and grow to successfully compete. Without profit, shareholders will find a better use for their money. Without profit, wages stagnate, and the best employees leave for greener pastures. Without profit, there is no survival. Samuel Gompers, labor union leader and founder of the American Federation of Labor (the AFL in AFL-CIO), believed the worst crime against working people was a company that failed to operate at a profit.

The greatest battle of the twentieth century did not take place on any battlefield; it took place in the markets, as capitalism and communism fought for supremacy. While both systems have flaws, those flaws are really human flaws, and communism simply exposed far more human flaws than capitalism.

We take capitalism for granted in capitalist countries, though many Christians aren't very comfortable with it. They hear the denunciations of materialism from the pulpit (and rightly so), but they fail to recognize the difference between materialism and capitalism.

Capitalism is a system that enables people to use money as a tool to find their calling to a degree that no other system has been able to match. *Materialism* is a disease that causes us to want money and possessions to an unhealthy degree. Because capitalism works better than any other system to provide the most material goods for the most people, capitalism is incorrectly viewed as the main cause of materialism. Believing that the cure for materialism is to eliminate capitalism is like believing that the cure for food poisoning is to eliminate food.

In order for capitalism to work, it needs some things that Christians hold in high esteem – cooperation, self-sacrifice, delayed gratification, risk-taking based on hope and faith, not to mention the rule of law and a stable home life.

Capitalism enables the creation of wealth better than any other system yet devised. While capitalism can create a greater disparity between rich and poor, it's important to remember that the poor in capitalist countries are still far better off than the poor under any other economic system. And there is greater opportunity to work your way out of poverty under capitalism than under any other system.

Following World War II, Korea, which had been under Japanese control for 35 years, was temporarily partitioned, with the Soviet Union overseeing the north and the U.S. overseeing the south. The refusal of the Soviets to proceed with reunification led to the Korean War.

Following the war, both North and South Korea were economically devastated. South Korea had less territory, a larger population, and no natural resources. The per capita GDP of both countries remained roughly the same for the next 20 years and was about $2,700 in 1972.

Over the next four decades, as capitalism and communism became more firmly established in each country, the virtues of capitalism became obvious. In 2014, the per capita GDP of South Korea was $33,770. The per capita GDP of North Korea was $1,800, one-third less than it was in 1972. In 2014 alone, South Korea produced 4.5 million cars. From 1994 to the present, an estimated 4.5 million North Koreans, some 20% of their population, have died of starvation. During that period, capitalist America provided 2.4 million tons of food aid; capitalist South Korea provided 3.3 million tons.

In his book, *Money, Greed, and God: Why Capitalism is the Solution and not the Problem*, Jay W. Richards says Christians' perspective of capitalism is distorted by eight myths:

- The Nirvana Myth (contrasting capitalism with an unrealizable ideal rather than actual alternatives)
- The Piety Myth (looking only at good intentions but not at unintended consequences)

- The Zero-Sum Game Myth (believing all trade requires a winner and a loser)
- The Materialist Myth (believing that wealth isn't created, but merely transferred)
- The Greed Myth (believing the essence of capitalism is greed)
- The Usury Myth (believing that working with money is inherently immoral and charging interest is always exploitative)
- The Artsy Myth (confusing aesthetic judgments with economic arguments)
- The Freeze-Frame Myth (taking the present situation and extrapolating it out into the indefinite future)

Milton Friedman was one of our greatest economists. While traveling to China in the 1970s, he visited a worksite where a new canal was being built. He was shocked to see that, instead of modern tractors and earth movers, the workers had shovels. He asked why there were so few machines. The government bureaucrat explained: "You don't understand. This is a jobs program." To which Friedman replied: "Oh, I thought you were trying to build a canal. If it's jobs you want, then you should give these workers spoons, not shovels."

Because capitalism is the only system yet devised that can create real sustainable wealth, it's also the only real cure for widespread generational poverty. Jobs that consume more wealth than they create will not survive in a capitalist system. However, the vibrancy of capitalism enables new jobs to be created to replace those that are eliminated. In other systems, the jobs ultimately die when the entire system dies.

The intrinsic value of work is that it provides the worker a sense of purpose by providing goods and services that benefit people. The economic value of work is that the benefit that others receive exceeds, if only slightly, the benefit the worker receives. The intrinsic and economic benefits must both be in their proper balance for a job to continue to exist.

If a minimum wage is higher than the economic benefit created by the work, the job will be eliminated for the simple reason that it loses money. If there's no intrinsic benefit to the job, like workers trying to dig a canal with spoons, they'll seek out some kind of work that actually improves the human condition as well as their own.

Frederick Herzberg was an American psychologist who greatly influenced business management with what is generally referred to as the Two-Factor Theory. Herzberg's theory states that people aren't content with satisfaction at the lower levels of Maslow's hierarchy of needs. Individuals will also seek gratification of higher-level psychological needs related to achievement, recognition, responsibility, advancement, and the nature of the work itself.

Two-factor theory distinguishes between:

- **Motivators** (challenging work, recognition, responsibility, achievement) that give positive satisfaction arising from intrinsic conditions of the work itself, and
- **Hygiene factors** (status, job security, salary, fringe benefits, work conditions) that do not give positive satisfaction, though their absence results in dissatisfaction. These factors are extrinsic to the work itself.

Essentially, hygiene factors are necessary to prevent an employee from becoming dissatisfied. Motivation factors are needed to motivate an employee to higher performance. Herzberg further classified workers' actions and how and why they do them. If you perform a work-related action because you *have* to, then that's classed as movement; if you perform a work-related action because you *want* to, then that's classed as motivation.

What is the environment where you work? If the hygiene factors are lacking or inadequate, it can be easy to feel dissatisfied. In such an environment, morale is low and turnover is high. Businesses that don't provide a minimum level of hygiene factors don't stay in business for long.

When a business is just starting up, the environment may be one where the hygiene factors are low, but the motivators are high. Hygiene factors are low because money is tight in most start-ups. The company can't offer security yet, but what they can offer is plenty of opportunity. It can be an exciting environment where everyone is enthused at the prospect of building something from scratch as a team. That enthusiasm and dedication should translate into profits at some point, and at that point the employer needs to raise the hygiene factors to an acceptable level.

Old school business thinking was that as long as the business took care of the hygiene factors, it was up to the employees to find their own motivation. If management focused more on people than numbers, an unproductive environment could result. The main reason people stay in such jobs is that the hygiene factors there are better than the hygiene factors elsewhere. People get used to a certain level of salaries and benefits, and they're reluctant to give some of that up for intangibles like recognition and achievement.

The goal is to have a work environment that offers both the requisite level of hygiene factors and as many motivators as possible. What many business managers fail to recognize is that the way to get workers to be their most productive is to pay them enough so that money is not an issue (which doesn't mean paying them more than anyone else or paying the employee as much as they demand) and then to provide as many motivators as possible.

To help get the proper perspective of money as a motivator, consider this scenario. At your place of employment, you feel you're well paid for the work you do. However, you just found out that two of your co-workers, neither of whom is more productive than you are, both earn more than you do. Would that news make you suddenly dissatisfied with your level of pay? What if you found out that those two co-workers were more satisfied with their jobs than you are, based on a survey all the workers completed? Would you care? That bit of information would be unlikely to raise your level of dissatisfaction.

The scenario just described illustrates a point - the best motivators are the ones that have no limits. When someone finds out that co-workers are paid more, they become dissatisfied because they believe that others' higher income must come at their own expense. When someone finds out that co-workers are more satisfied in their jobs, they don't become dissatisfied because satisfaction isn't a finite resource; it can be created in infinite quantities by those who will benefit most from its creation.

We tend to think of those hygiene factors as motivators in part because of the Industrial Revolution. Before the Industrial Revolution, work was arduous and often dangerous, but for the most part it wasn't routine. Two-thirds of the population worked in agriculture prior to the Industrial Revolution, and that work had many drawbacks, but at least there was a certain variety to it.

Prior to the Industrial Revolution, there were no assembly lines. With the advent of the modern factory, tasks were broken down to their smallest elements, and workers would perform those smallest elements continuously. If you worked at a Ford assembly plant in 1920, you could take pride that you were part of the team that built the Model T, the car that put America on wheels. However, your workday consisted of attaching the front bumper on the driver's side as each car came down the line. Your work involved six separate steps and had to be completed in 42 seconds because that was the pace of the moving assembly line. By the end of the year, you would have attached 171,428 bumpers to 171,428 Model Ts. Work like that required a lot of outside direction and supervision. No one can stay self-motivated performing the same routine 86 times an hour, 8 hours a day, 250 days a year.

Non-routine jobs are far more common today. The pace of change requires jobs to evolve continuously to keep up with new technologies and competition. The push for productivity now has workers multi-tasking, as opposed to breaking work down into smaller and smaller increments. The variety of activities in the average workday today makes it easier for workers to maintain interest in their work. The number of workers putting in 10 and 12 hour workdays may be the result of the push for more productivity, but they couldn't be productive for 10 or 12 hours a day unless the work was able to hold their interest for that long a period.

One of the great motivators is autonomy. We all want to think we're the ones who decide what we're going to do. If you're a parent, you've probably used an If-Then scenario with your child at some time. They can be stated positively or negatively, as a carrot or a stick: "If you clean your room, we can go get ice cream. If you don't clean your room, you can't play any video games." If-Then rewards, and especially punishments, are perceived as reducing one's autonomy.

Autonomy is one of those intrinsic motivators. Intrinsic motivators are delicate things. They can be damaged by, of all things, extrinsic rewards. Bobby Jones was one of the greatest golfers of all time, winning thirteen major tournaments. He also co-founded Augusta National and the Masters Tournament. He was a lawyer by profession and only played golf as an amateur. When asked why he never turned pro, he replied, "When you play for money, it's not love anymore." The lesson of Bobby Jones is: when people are doing something because of intrinsic motivators, don't muck it up by offering extrinsic rewards. You'll only hurt their performance.

Extrinsic rewards, like money, can send two seemingly contradictory signals at the same time. The first signal is that the task you're performing is valuable and that someone wants to demonstrate appreciation of your performing it with financial compensation. The second signal is that the task you're performing is inherently undesirable and that the only way to entice you to perform this undesirable task is to offer you financial compensation. We prefer the first signal simply because there's an intrinsic element to it: the recognition and appreciation of our performing a task well.

Extrinsic rewards, like money, tend to have a more addictive quality, compared to intrinsic rewards. We easily get used to whatever level of material comfort we currently enjoy, a trait known as adaptation. If we suddenly had to take a pay cut of 10%, we would experience symptoms similar to drug withdrawal. We're capable of adapting to the change for the worse, but we certainly don't like it; furthermore, it can cloud our attitude toward our work. Also, once we get paid for doing something, it's unlikely we'll ever be willing to do it again for free. In such a case, we're willing to give up the good vibes of doing something for the joy of it if we're no longer getting paid to do it. It feels as if we're giving away something of value to someone who should be paying for it.

In order to feel motivated, we need to feel that the work we're performing has some importance, and we also need to feel a certain sense of urgency about it. A sense of urgency and importance isn't hard to come by if you're the attending physician in a hospital emergency room; it may be harder to generate those feelings when you're reviewing expense reports at an insurance company.

There's a reason why every task at work needs to be done. If you don't see how your task fits into the big picture at work, you owe it to yourself to find out how the work you do makes a positive difference in people's lives. Your boss, if he/she is worthy of the position, knows you deserve such knowledge and that such knowledge can be a great motivator.

Your boss should also recognize that once you feel a sense of urgency and importance to your work, the best thing to do is free you to get the work done in the best way you see fit. If you're properly motivated about the purpose of your work, you're also properly motivated to do that work to the best of your ability and as efficiently as possible.

The words "work" and "toil" are mentioned over 480 times in the Bible. God wants us to work, He expects us to work, and He promises to reward us for our work.

There is, or should be, a spiritual aspect to our work, even in the most secular of occupations. Work is not a burden from God; it's a gift from God. Work is a gift from God that enables us to:

- Serve others
- Be self-sufficient to our own needs
- Support our families
- Earn money to give to others
- Demonstrate love of God and our neighbor.

One of the best ways to praise God and thank Him for our blessings is to do our work to the best of our ability, whatever our work may be.

KILLING 'EM WITH KINDNESS

Who decides how much you'll be paid? That question may generate a lot of different answers from different people. Those who are self-employed may say that they themselves decide how much they're paid, based on how hard they work and how well they control costs. Those who work in the private sector may say that their pay was negotiated within a range determined by the employer for that particular position. Those who work in the public sector may say that their pay is based on specific pay grades for specific positions and is not subject to negotiation.

One answer that almost no one would give, though it would be appropriate in all these examples is, "The market decides how much I'll be paid." For the self-employed person, the market will quickly determine how much it's willing to pay for the product or service offered. Pay will be the product of the ability to meet demand while controlling costs. For the private sector employee, their competence in the current position determines where in the salary range they'll fall and how quickly they'll get to move to a better position with a higher salary. For the public sector employee, tax rates, skill sets, and competition from the private sector will all have an effect on pay scales.

There's one group that's seemingly exempt from market forces determining pay levels. It's the group at the bottom of the pay levels – those earning the minimum wage.

No one questions the good intentions of those who advocate for an increase in the minimum wage. No one questions the good intentions of those who want to help those who have less. One of the most powerful tools we have for turning good intentions into results is money. But money, more than any other tool, can create unintended and harmful consequences to those who are supposed to be helped. This chapter takes a look at some of those unintended consequences and how we might do a better job of actually helping those who need our help – how we can stop killing 'em with kindness.

Congress established the federal minimum wage with the Fair Labor Standards Act of 1938. The stated purpose of the act was to raise the wages of the lowest-paid workers. The real purpose of the act was to raise the wages of union workers.

Then, as now, unions were heavily involved in politics. By raising the minimum wage for unskilled workers, one consequence (this one intentional) was to raise the wages for skilled workers, most of whom were union members at that time. Unions, which strongly backed the idea of a minimum wage, were perceived as championing even those who weren't in a union. The unintended consequence though, was a rise in unemployment among unskilled workers as they got priced out of the labor market. Making matters worse, those who got priced out of the labor market in the late 1930s were disproportionately black or other minorities.

At a Senate hearing in 1957, then-Senator John F. Kennedy addressed an NAACP official regarding Kennedy's support for the minimum wage:

"Of course, having on the market a rather large source of cheap labor depresses wages outside of that group, too – the wages of the white worker who has to compete. And when an employer can substitute a colored worker at a lower wage – and there are, as you pointed out, these hundreds of thousands looking for decent work – it affects the whole wage structure of an area, doesn't it?"

Kennedy's support for an increase in the minimum wage had nothing to do with improving the lot of those who would be affected by an increase. His statement, in fact, acknowledges that an increase in the minimum wage would likely have a negative effect on those workers. His purpose in supporting an increase in the minimum wage was to increase the wages of his constituency – white union workers in Massachusetts.

No one would advocate today that the *intentions* of raising the minimum wage have any racist aspects to them. However, if one were to look only at the *consequences* of raising the minimum wage, it would be hard to ignore the racially biased results.

A study by labor economists at Miami University and the University of Texas looked at the 41% hike in the minimum wage between 2007 and 2009. For white males ages 16 to 24, each 10% increase in the minimum wage decreased employment 2.5%; for Hispanic males, the figure was 1.2%; for black males, it was 6.5%.

One of the biggest stated motives of those who advocate a higher minimum wage is raising poor working families out of poverty. Such motives assume two things: raising the minimum wage won't result in increased unemployment among those working families, and working families comprise the bulk of those making the minimum wage.

One-third of minimum wage workers are in families in the top half of the income distribution. These workers are typically young and are living with their parents. Most important, they don't have to support anyone, even themselves, on their earnings.

Only around 5% of hourly workers make the minimum wage; the percentage of the entire labor force making the minimum wage is far less than that. Most are under age 25, and two-thirds of them work part-time. They're also rarely the sole breadwinner in their household. The beneficiary of a rising minimum wage is more likely to be the kid down the street from me in my nice suburban enclave, not the single mom in the inner city. A rising minimum wage mostly reduces that single mom's job prospects.

In 1939, the year the federal minimum wage was established, 85% of those making the minimum wage were in poor families. By 1969 that figure had dropped to 23%; by 2003 it was 9%. The great majority of the poor make more than the minimum wage, and the great majority of those earning the minimum wage aren't poor.

Economist Henry Hazlitt, who wrote about business and economics for *The Wall Street Journal, Newsweek, The New York Times*, and many other publications, said, "You cannot make a man worth a given amount by making it illegal to offer him anything less." Markets, not governments, ultimately determine labor's worth.

Here's a hypothetical illustration of the unintended consequences of raising the minimum wage.

I manage a fast food restaurant in the inner city. There are twenty-five employees; fifteen make the minimum wage, and ten make more. Seventeen employees are under age 21, and they all work part-time. Six employees are full-time, and two of them are assistant managers and the main breadwinners in their households.

The current minimum wage is $7.50 per hour and total payroll (excluding me and including employer's share of FICA/Medicare) is $7,583 per week. The minimum wage has just been increased to $9.00 per hour, a 20% increase. All of the minimum wage employees and four of the other employees will get mandated raises to the new $9.00 per hour rate. Weekly payroll is estimated to rise to $8,805 per week.

Our customers are extremely price sensitive, so prices can only rise about 2% to cover the higher labor costs. Optimistically assuming the price increase doesn't cost us any business, revenues would increase $482 per week, leaving $740 per week in additional expenses uncovered.

Including FICA/Medicare, the minimum wage employee now costs $9.67 per hour. The $740 in uncovered expenses works out to 76.5 hours per week. I now have to reduce the total hours worked in the restaurant by that number. I have no choice. Prices can't rise any more without actually decreasing income, and there are no other areas to reduce expenses. *I have to let three of my part-time people go.*

Those who passed the increase in the minimum wage will pat themselves on the back for raising the wages of sixteen of these employees. I'm glad these employees are now earning more, too. However, I also see the unintended consequences of this action, which include:

- Price increases for all of our customers, regardless of their ability to pay;
- The workforce was reduced, but not the workload. Employees now have to do 15% more work every hour to offset the reduced workforce;
- Three people, or 12% of the workforce, are now unemployed.

I also see the faces of Darius, Maria, and Steve, the three young people I had to let go. Their prospects for getting another job are slim. What just happened in this restaurant is happening all over the neighborhood. The jobs they're qualified to do are being squeezed out everywhere by the higher wages. The young and the unskilled need to grab the bottom rung of the economic ladder. They can't do that if the rung is raised too high.

Here's the epilogue. Steve had to move back with his Mom, and she's supporting him while he tries to find another job. Maria was helping to support her family. She's no longer able to do that, and her situation was made worse when her mother was demoted from assistant manager at another fast food restaurant to assume the duties of the laid-off workers there. Finally, Darius, who was using his earnings to pay his way through technical school, had to quit school. He's now unemployed, out of school, and he's begun hanging out with the wrong crowd. The unintended consequences have only just begun.

Minimum wage laws are a method the government uses to shift wealth to the poor through the private sector. While this method may raise the standard of living for some, for far too many it makes a bad situation much worse. If you look at the overall situation of the twenty-five employees in the previous illustration, the sixteen employees who got raises also had their workloads increased by a similar percentage; so, in reality, their pay/work ratio is unchanged. Even if those sixteen employees see the change as a net positive, it's more than offset by the pain inflicted on the three employees who were let go. The goal of raising the minimum wage may have been to improve the lot of these people, but the result was a net increase in misery, and an unfairly distributed one at that.

When efforts to improve the lot of the poor by manipulating the private sector fail, the next step is to use the public sector to effect change.

The World Giving Index (WGI) ranks 153 countries on how charitable their populations are. The U.S. ranked first in 2013; our score of 61% was the highest on record. The index measures charitable donations, as well as donations of time and helping strangers.

One of the more interesting findings of the WGI survey is that, around the globe, happiness was seen as a greater influence on giving money than was wealth. Giving from the heart makes one happy, which prompts even more giving. God loves a cheerful giver, and cheerful people love to give.

People love to give from the heart; they don't like to be compelled to give. Nobody likes an aggressive panhandler. When the government raises taxes for the purpose of wealth redistribution, taxpayers can feel like they're being compelled to give by an aggressive panhandler, one backed by the force of the IRS.

There's an inverse correlation between tax rates and charitable giving rates. People feel they have only so much they can give away, and both taxes and charity feel like they're giving money away. The higher the tax rates, the less people feel they have left to give to charity. Conversely, the lower the tax rates, the more they feel they can give to charity. Higher tax rates may encourage those in the highest tax brackets to make more tax deductible charitable donations, but the overall effect of higher tax rates is to reduce the total giving to charity by all taxpayers.

Compulsory taxation for benevolent purposes (defined here as anti-poverty/welfare programs) has unintended consequences. It creates resentment of the tax collector, in most cases the federal government. It creates resentment of the recipient, which can lead to a caricature of the recipient as an able-bodied parasite. Also, and perhaps, most important, compulsory taxation for benevolent purposes creates the illusion that you already gave at the office.

If someone is paying a 25% tax rate, it may be that less than 1/10th of that money is going toward benevolent purposes. However, it *feels* like much more is going to those purposes (We tend to overestimate how much of our taxes go to programs we dislike.), so charitable giving is reduced by more than is collected in taxes.

Part of the pain of the higher tax rate is transferred to charitable organizations through reduced giving. Charities are less able to help people, who then become more dependent on government support, thus requiring even higher tax rates. And since charities do a much better job than governments in getting the most for their money, the real victims of higher tax rates are the people who are supposed to be helped.

A half-century has now passed since Lyndon Johnson's declaration of a "War on Poverty". Between 1959 and the 1965 start of the War on Poverty, the poverty rate in the U.S. had declined from 22% to 15%. The poverty rate has never been below 12% at any time since the War on Poverty began. The 2010 U.S. census declared that 15.1% of the population lived in poverty. A half-century of effort by federal, state, and local governments to reduce poverty has yielded absolutely nothing. Their efforts have, in fact, only made the situation far worse.

The above figures are based on *absolute poverty*, which measures poverty against a fixed standard. While adjusted for inflation, absolute poverty measurements have a certain consistency over time. Even though efforts to reduce poverty have been a dismal failure as measured by levels of absolute poverty, those who deny their failure will defend current anti-poverty programs by looking at *relative poverty*.

The United Nations, the European Union, and those on the left in the U.S. prefer to cite relative poverty statistics. They cite economist John Kenneth Galbraith, who said in 1958, "People are poverty stricken when their income, *even if adequate for survival*, falls markedly behind that of their community." *(emphasis mine)*

Under the definition of relative poverty, if everyone's real income increases, but the income distribution stays the same, the rate of relative poverty will also stay the same. By this definition, there will always be people living in poverty, unless all incomes are the same. Using relative poverty as a measure, someone making

$100,000 would be considered poor if the average income in their community were $1 million.

Because relative poverty is really a measure of income inequality, one way to lower the relative poverty rate is to lower the incomes of the wealthy. If economic events cause more harm to the wealthy than the poor, relative poverty can drop even if everyone has less money, including the poor. Likewise, if everyone is getting richer, but the rich are getting richer faster than the poor (which is almost always the case), relative poverty will increase while absolute poverty is falling.

Winston Churchill said, "The inherent vice of capitalism is the unequal sharing of blessings; the inherent virtue of socialism is the equal sharing of miseries." Since it's impossible in a capitalist society to effect an equal sharing of blessings, otherwise well-meaning people are happy to effect an equal sharing of miseries. Yet, as history has proven through absolute poverty rates, they've succeeded only in increasing the misery of the non-poor, not in reducing the misery of the poor.

Mary Harris "Mother" Jones was a labor and community organizer in the early twentieth century. She cofounded the Industrial Workers of the World, an industrial union formed to overturn capitalism and wage labor. *Mother Jones* magazine is named after her.

Mother Jones is credited with saying, "My business is to comfort the afflicted and afflict the comfortable." I've heard this quote repeated many times by politicians and, unfortunately, by some clergy. It may seem a noble cause at first glance. However, such a "business" is in reality a scam because a never-ending need for that person's services is created. The comfortable become the afflicted, and the afflicted become the comfortable;

then the process has to be reversed. It's a never ending cycle that guarantees lifetime employment. It's made even easier because the same person doing the afflicting and comforting also determines who is comfortable and who is afflicted. It's nice work if you can get it.

Compulsory wealth redistribution by governments is nothing less than afflicting the comfortable and comforting the afflicted. When such goals become government policy, everyone will try to be classified as afflicted and to avoid at all costs being classified as comfortable. It becomes in everyone's self-interest to adopt a victim mentality.

Karl Marx advocated, "From each according to his ability to each according to his needs." That policy guaranteed that everyone would demonstrate minimum ability and maximum need, leading to the inevitable collapse of communism. Wealth redistribution is a simple rephrasing of Marx: From each according to his comfort level to each according to his affliction.

The poor may be miserable on a relative basis, but on an absolute basis their situation is less grim. The U.S. Census Bureau points out:

- 46% of poor households own their own home. The average "poor" home has three bedrooms, one-and-a-half baths, a garage, and a porch/patio.
- 76% of poor households have air conditioning.
- The average poor American has more living space than the average non-poor resident of Paris, London, Vienna, Athens, or Tokyo.
- Nearly 75% of poor households own a car; 30% own two or more cars.
- 97% have a color TV; over half have more than one.
- 78% have a DVD player; 62% have cable or satellite.

- 73% have a microwave; 35% have an automatic dishwasher.

Based on this data, the middle-class household I grew up in fifty years ago would have to be a lot nicer to be the average poor household of today.

Here are U.S. census figures on who lives in poverty:

- 5.8% of people in married families
- 26.6% of people in single-parent households
- 19.1% of people living alone
- 9.9% of white persons
- 12.1% of Asian persons
- 26.6% of Hispanic persons
- 28.4% of black persons
- 22% of people under age 18
- 13.7% of people 19-64
- 9% of people 65 and older

The largest disparity in these numbers is between the poverty rates of people in married families and people in single-parent households. When broken down by single-parent households headed by women, the disparity is even worse; 47.1% of people living in such households live in poverty. Those households are more likely to have an above-average number of children and to be black or Hispanic, raising the numbers for those groups, too.

Some other statistics of federal welfare are revealing:

- Once they started receiving welfare benefits, husbands reduced working hours an average of 9%; wives reduced working hours an average of 20%; young males reduced working hours an average of 33%; singles reduced working hours an average of 43%.

- Every dollar of subsidy leads to a reduction of labor and earnings of 80 cents.
- Among low-income women ages 14-22, a 10% increase in welfare benefits increased out-of-wedlock births 12%; a 50% increase in welfare benefits increased out-of-wedlock births 43%.
- In 1965, 24% of black infants and 3% of white infants were born to single mothers. In 2012, 72% of black infants, 67% of Native American infants, 54% of Hispanic infants, 29% of white infants, and 17% of Asian infants were born to single mothers. The total national average was 40.7%, or two infants out of every five.

Anthropologist Margaret Mead said that the ultimate test of any culture is whether it can successfully socialize men to willingly nurture their children. If the statistics above are any indication, we've been getting worse in this area for a half-century now.

Since 1965, access to birth control and the options available have increased dramatically. There are some twenty different birth control methods covered under the Affordable Care Act. Based on the ease of obtaining birth control today compared to 1965, the rise in out-of-wedlock births is doubly alarming. Among other things, the rise in out-of-wedlock births at a time when birth control is easier than ever indicates most of these pregnancies were planned, or at least no reasonable effort was made to prevent them.

There are several overlapping explanations for the increase. There are perceived financial incentives, in the form of increased welfare benefits, for having additional children. (The absence of the father actually makes it easier to obtain such benefits.) Young, single females, especially those in poor, single-parent families, yearn for someone to love and to love them, and if they can't find one, the next best thing is to make one. Finally, there's no longer a stigma to having a child out-of-wedlock. Husbands aren't needed; a babydaddy will do.

One of the unintended consequences of the increase in fatherless families and the government support of them has been the marginalization of the father in the wider culture, but in some minority cultures especially.

A young man needs to learn his responsibilities and be made to meet those responsibilities. It's a test of our culture, as Margaret Mead stated. Young men, especially those who grew up with a shortage of positive male role models, don't instinctively know their responsibilities. It's up to society to make sure they know, and we fail in that mission when we assume those responsibilities for him instead of teaching him.

Supporting a fatherless family through welfare may seem like the right thing to do, but it degrades the role of father and deprives the father of the opportunity to become a better man. As Don Corleone said, "A man who doesn't spend time with his family can never be a real man."

In 1994, President Clinton launched the National Partners in Homeownership, a private-public cooperative with the singular goal of raising the homeownership rate from 64% to 70% by the year 2000.

The goal of bumping homeownership a mere six points may seem a modest one, and the goal of increasing the percentage of minority homeowners may seem a noble one, but the percentage of homeowners had hovered in the low-to-mid sixties for decades, and moving it would require some systemic changes.

There are two methods to increase homeownership. One method is to increase the number of people who meet the existing standards to qualify to buy a home, which includes having sufficient financial assets and income, plus a decent credit score. This method requires education and time and may not be very effective. The second method is to lower the existing standards to qualify for a mortgage. The federal government, with the support of quasi-public mortgage companies Fannie Mae and Freddie Mac, opted for the latter.

Underwriting standards were lowered across the board for mortgages to qualify more people. Those who objected to the lower standards largely kept silent for fear of a racial discrimination charge.

In the past, if you went to your local bank for a mortgage, they made sure you were qualified to pay it back. They did so because they were lending you their money, or more specifically the money of their depositors. In the past, the originator of the mortgage maintained a stake in the mortgage, too.

In this new era, lenders could off-load any risky loans to the government through Fannie Mae and Freddie Mac. Fannie and Freddie made money on these loans by bundling them into mortgage-backed securities and selling them through Wall Street firms to institutions and individuals looking for income.

Many, if not most of these loans would have qualified as subprime under the old underwriting standards. Even with the relaxed standards, subprime mortgage origination grew from $35 billion to $125 billion between 1994 and 1997. By late 1995, nearly one in five mortgages qualified as subprime. By 2008, $3.3 *trillion* in toxic mortgages were on the books, nearly half of them purchased or guaranteed by Fannie or Freddie, both of which were private for-profit companies that also had government protection from insolvency.

Investors loved the high yield of mortgage-backed securities, especially since the risk ratings on them were very low compared to the yield. Money poured in to finance mortgages, which led to even lower underwriting standards and very aggressive marketing to almost anyone who could fog a mirror. Many people qualified for mortgages without having to show proof of income, assets, or even employment.

Subprime mortgages were aggressively marketed to minorities, particularly Hispanics and African-Americans. These instruments were devised with the knowledge that their intended market had, on average, a sixth-grade reading level. People who previously sold cars and cell phones were particularly good at pushing subprime mortgages to this demographic.

The Center for Responsible Lending's research shows that African-American and Hispanic borrowers were about 30% more likely to get higher rate subprime loans than white borrowers with similar risk characteristics. Making it easier for minorities to get a loan isn't much help if the lender exploits their minority status by grossly overcharging them.

Although many mortgages written during this period were subprime mortgages for first-time minority buyers, the majority were for cash-out refinancings, which allowed borrowers to take the paper gains generated by the housing bubble. Two-thirds of the proceeds from these loans went to personal consumption, home improvements, and credit card debt.

In addition to not knowing the terms of their loans, many of these first-time home buyers didn't know the other costs in time and money required to maintain a home. Repairs and maintenance used to be done by a landlord; now it was their responsibility. Many didn't have the expertise or the funds to properly maintain their homes, and the condition and value of the homes declined as a result.

The decline in home values resulting from deferred maintenance was nothing compared to the plunge that occurred when people started defaulting on their mortgages. For some, the monthly mortgage payment itself couldn't be covered. For some, it could be covered until one of the breadwinners became unemployed. For some, a balloon payment couldn't be met, triggering default. And for some, the plunge in home values put them so far "underwater" they decided to just walk away from the whole thing.

In addition to a lack of education and experience in home buying, many of the people who ended up in default on their mortgages were the victims of misplaced trust.

In the past, when someone went to a lender, they assumed the lender would determine what a safe amount to borrow was. After all, the lender was putting its own money on the line; surely they wouldn't loan more than they felt the borrower could repay. However, because the "lenders" in these cases were merely brokers paid to close the deal and pass the actual loan on to another entity, their incentive was not to make good loans, but to make big loans, and the more the better. There were doubtless many conversations between husband and wife that went something like this:

Wife: *Are you sure we can afford this monthly payment? I'm really not comfortable with this big a bill every month. I don't see how we can pay it and all our other bills with what we make now.*

Husband: *Don't worry, honey. If the mortgage was more than we could afford, they wouldn't have approved us. They have to look out for their own interests, too. They know more about this stuff than we do. If they say we can afford it, that's good enough for me.*

While the initial notion of giving more minorities a chance to participate in the American dream was a noble one, it was almost immediately co-opted by parties that saw a way to make a ton of money from it. These ranged from Fannie and Freddie to the big firms of Wall Street to members of Congress to commercial banks large and small to sleazy, smooth-talking brokers.

In the end, almost everybody took a major hit when the housing bubble burst. The demand created by the explosion of subprime mortgages led to a housing bubble. When the bubble burst, it not only ravaged the housing market, it created the financial crisis of 2008, which nearly collapsed the entire world financial system. A complete recovery from this whole disastrous episode is years, if not decades away.

So what was the final tally from the government's attempt to artificially increase the homeowner population? Excluding the subsequent recession and the millions of jobs it cost, since 2005, 22% of Hispanics have lost their homes to foreclosure; for African-Americans, the number is 17%; for whites, it's 9%. Home value depreciation was also far worse in minority neighborhoods, as a higher percentage of those homes went back on the market after foreclosures, further depressing prices. Finally, the Great Recession triggered by the housing debacle caused wealth losses of 66% for Hispanics, 54% for Asians, 53% for African-Americans, and 13% for whites. Since home equity is a higher percentage of wealth for these minorities, plunging home values hit them hardest.

Not only have those who were supposed to be helped by looser lending practices been the ones hurt most by its failure, their pain may go on for some time. Having owned a home and lost it is psychologically harder than never owning a home in the first place. For almost everyone who lost their home through foreclosure, it will be years before they'll again qualify for a mortgage.

Finally, the percentage of minorities who are homeowners is less today than it was in 1994 when President Clinton launched the National Partners for Homeownership.

A few years ago, *National Geographic* magazine ran a piece on Hispaniola, the Caribbean island that contains Haiti in the west and the Dominican Republic in the east. One of the photographs was an aerial photo of the border between the two countries, which ran through a mountainous section of the island.

Despite no evidence of human presence in the photo, the location of the border was unmistakable. The Dominican side of the border was covered in a lush rainforest. The Haitian side resembled the semi-arid desert areas of Mexico. There was hardly a healthy plant growing in Haiti, right up to the border. The stark contrast between the two sides of the border is the result of deforestation by the Haitians, and not by any natural occurrence. Haiti was not a proper steward of its resources and lost them as a result.

That photo was an accurate representation of what Haiti has become. A place that could be vibrant with growth has become a place where mere survival is a longshot.

Haiti's per capita GDP is about $1,300, by far the lowest in the western hemisphere and 209th out of 229 countries in the world. Official unemployment is 41%, and more than two-thirds of the labor force do not have formal jobs. Eighty percent of the population lives below the poverty line, and 54% live in abject poverty, according to the *World Factbook*. Three-quarters of the population lives on less than $2 per day.

Haiti's trade deficit amounts to 41% of GDP. Foreign aid makes up 30-40% of the government's budget. The World Bank estimates that 80-90% of Haiti's college graduates live abroad, and their remittances back home amount to more than half of the country's GDP. Tourism brings in roughly $200 million per year, though it's only one-fifth the tourism revenue of neighboring Dominican Republic.

Why is Haiti such an ongoing basket case? For decades now, governments, churches, and charities around the world have flooded Haiti with money and volunteers to help raise the Haitian people out of poverty. For all the aid and effort, Haiti continues to fall farther behind the rest of the world every year. Why?

One reason that such aid, be it foreign or domestic, fails to accomplish its goals is that the givers evaluate the value of their aid/charity by the short-term rewards they receive through service (warm fuzzies), instead of evaluating the value by the *long-term* benefits received by the served.

Note the emphasis on long-term benefits. A short-term benefit is giving them a fish. A long-term benefit is teaching them to fish. Giving them a fish makes the giver feel good; teaching them to fish is a lot of work, and the rewards are a long time coming. Giving them a fish is OK if it's made contingent on their learning how to fish ASAP. Of course, that requirement also requires a commitment to teach them how to fish.

Robert D. Lupton is the founder and president of FCS Urban Ministries in Atlanta. His book, *Toxic Charity*, is a compilation of his observations over four decades in urban and foreign ministries. At the center of Lupton's recommendations is his *Oath for Compassionate Service*:

- Never do for the poor what they have (or could have) the capacity to do for themselves.
- Limit one-way giving to emergency situations.
- Strive to empower the poor through employment, lending, and investing, using grants sparingly to reinforce achievements.
- Subordinate self-interest to the needs of those being served.
- Listen closely to those you seek to help, especially to what isn't being said – unspoken feelings may contain essential clues to effective service.
- Above all, do no harm.

This last item is violated by almost all foreign aid and charitable efforts. It's certainly not their intention to inflict harm, but they also can't ignore the fact that most aid and charity efforts overseas have a long-term detrimental effect on those who are supposedly being helped. Refusing to acknowledge the facts and change methods merely aligns intentions with consequences.

Churches and their mission groups, for all their good intentions, are some of the worst when it comes to harming those they're trying to help. Instead of empowering the locals, relieving poverty, or even making better Christians of those making the trip, the results are more typically a deepened dependency on charity and an eroded work ethic on the part of those receiving the aid.

When you look at the time, effort, and expense of sending a mission group from the U.S. to Africa (a favorite destination), it would be far more efficient and effective to send a couple of trained people to show the locals how to dig a well, build a school, etc., perhaps provide some seed money to get the project going, and then let those who will receive the benefit take over once they learn what to do.

A typical rebuttal to such a suggestion from people connected with church-affiliated mission groups is that such an arrangement doesn't benefit the members of their congregation. *So What?* If it's a *real* mission, it doesn't exist for the benefit of the missionaries. If helping out means that the intended beneficiaries are made worse so the missionaries can feel good about their Christian charity, it would be better if those missionaries did nothing at all.

When speaking candidly, local liaisons for charitable missions will readily admit that mission trips destroy the initiative of the recipients. Mission groups arrive with regularity, so there's no incentive to build something on their own. They'll take the charity and smile for photos, but they resent being turned into beggars.

There's nothing wrong with wanting to give, and we all know it's more blessed to give than to receive. But charity isn't the same as gift giving. In charity, the giver becomes superior, in a position of control. For his part, the recipient becomes indebted, humiliated, and in a lower state than he was before.

James Baldwin, in referring to the changes brought about by the Civil Rights movement in America, said, "Nothing is more desirable than to be released from an affliction, but nothing is more frightening than to be divested of a crutch." As degrading as most charity is to the recipients and as much as they would rather rid themselves of the affliction of dependency, they're not likely to throw away the crutch; it's just too frightening. They'll smile, say thank you, and continue on their downward spiral. Robert Lupton chronicles the downward spiral thusly:

- Give once and you elicit appreciation.
- Give twice and you create anticipation.
- Give three times and you create expectation.
- Give four times and it becomes entitlement.
- Give five times and you establish dependency.

Microcredit has grown rapidly in recent years as one method of breaking the cycle of poverty exacerbated by charity alone. The pioneering of microcredit is credited to Dr. Mohammad Yunus, who began experimenting with lending to poor women in the village of Jobra, Bangladesh during his tenure as a professor of economics at Chittagong University in the 1970s. He would go on to found Grameen Bank in 1983 and win the Nobel Peace Prize in 2006.

Microcredit is the extension of very small loans to impoverished borrowers who typically lack collateral, steady employment, and a verifiable credit history. It's designed not only to support entrepreneurship and alleviate poverty, but also in many cases to empower women and uplift entire communities by extension. As of 2013, an estimated 86 million men and women held microloans totaling $43 billion. Grameen Bank reports repayment rates are between 95 and 98%.

For microcredit to be appropriate, clients must have the capacity to repay the loan under the terms provided.

Otherwise, clients may not be able to benefit from credit and risk being pushed into debt problems.

Microcredit may be inappropriate where conditions pose challenges to standard microcredit methodologies. Populations may pose problems that are geographically dispersed, nomadic, have a high incidence of debilitating illnesses (e.g., HIV/AIDS), depend on a single economic activity or single agricultural crop, or if they rely on barter rather than cash transactions. The presence of hyperinflation or the absence of law and order may stress the ability of microcredit to operate.

Rich countries have sent $2.3 *trillion* in aid to poor countries in the past fifty years. Almost without exception, the countries receiving aid are worse off now than they were fifty years ago in absolute terms, but they're certainly worse off in comparison to countries that had to rely on their own people to improve their standard of living.

One of the most admired (though fictional) characters in the Bible is the Good Samaritan. We all aspire to be like the Good Samaritan, coming to the rescue, helping those in need. No one was ever called a Good Samaritan without it being given and taken as a compliment. When we give to a charity, go on a mission trip, or have a clean-up day in the inner city, we see ourselves as Good Samaritans. And it feels good.

The situation the Good Samaritan found himself in was very different from what we see in inner cities and third world countries. The Good Samaritan was presented with a crisis – a man was severely beaten and robbed, and no one offered help. If the Samaritan didn't help, the man might die; he was already half dead, according to the parable.

The situations that prompt aid and charity are rarely crises; they're chronic, and chronic requires long-term solutions, not constant crisis management. If the problem in the parable were a chronic one of people being constantly beaten and robbed along that road, the solution would not have been to keep picking them up and bringing them to the inn. The solution would have been to hunt down the criminals and punish them. Treat the disease, not merely the symptoms.

The Good Samaritan also turned over the care of the beaten man to the innkeepers, and then he went on his way. His ability to help later was dependent on his ability to not be derailed by the crisis du jour. He most likely had business to conduct, and his ability to help in the future required him to take care of his own business first.

The Samaritan was also of a lower class. Jesus identifies the giver of aid as a Samaritan to make the point that class does not determine goodness. He didn't specifically identify anyone else in the parable. In situations where aid and charity are given, there's an implicit, if not explicit, recognition that the giver is somehow superior to the receiver, if for no other reason than their relative positions as giver and receiver.

Finally, the biggest difference between the Good Samaritan of the Bible and too many Good Samaritans of today – the Good Samaritan in the parable did no harm.

Daniel Patrick Moynihan was a U.S. Senator, sociologist, a U.N. Ambassador, and served in four presidential administrations from Kennedy through Ford. While working as Assistant Secretary of Labor in the Johnson administration, he issued a report titled, *The Negro Family: A Case for National Action*. Moynihan was vilified by many for stating in the report that the rising rate of out-of-wedlock births in the black population was a problem with long-term ramifications.

Moynihan was prophetic in his predictions that a rise in out-of-wedlock births would keep more African-Americans mired in poverty. He was also correct in his assessment that increasing welfare would reduce the man's role as breadwinner and, in turn, diminish him as a husband and father, straining the bonds of family. He advocated less welfare and more job training for black males in particular.

There is a term that was used frequently by President George W. Bush, but was actually coined by Daniel Moynihan in the 1960s – *the soft bigotry of low expectations*. Whenever it's assumed that a person or a group is incapable of accomplishing something, simply because they haven't yet accomplished it because it was never expected of them, the ones making the assumption are guilty of the soft bigotry of low expectations.

Every time we offer aid and charity to people who shouldn't need it, we diminish them as humans. Every time we do for someone what they can and should do for themselves, we steal from them the opportunity to grow in both the spiritual and secular realms. Every time we assume a person or a people can't rise to our level, we practice the soft bigotry of low expectations. If we believe we're all truly equal, we can practice that belief by giving *everyone* the opportunity to prove it.

FINANCIAL STABILITY IN YOUR HOUSE

Corporations live and die by financial statements. The numbers that appear on those statements determine stock prices, profitability, bonuses, and continued employment for top executives. The numbers are important enough that they have to be verified by independent auditors to prevent corporate insiders from "cooking the books".

The most basic, yet most important, financial statements are the *income statement* and the *balance sheet*. The income statement lists all income and expenses for the corporation over a certain period of time and calculates the profit or loss for the firm over that period. The balance sheet lists all assets and liabilities for the corporation at a given point in time. The assets minus the liabilities equal the net worth of the corporation; it's typically stated as stockholders' equity.

Corporations need to know their financial health, and these financial statements give them that information.

Households are no different. Every household needs to know how they're spending their income and whether spending exceeds income. They also need to know if they're becoming more or less wealthy over time.

Households don't have stockholders, employees, or customers, but in some ways their financial health is even more important than that of a corporation. The financial stability of a household affects the family that makes up that household. Financial instability can lead to the loss of the home through foreclosure or eviction. More critical, it can also demolish a marriage and inflict serious psychological harm on the children.

Financial order in your house enables you to fulfill your missions as a member of the household, be it a spouse, parent, neighbor, or citizen. Beyond taking care of the members of the household, financial stability enables the family to help others through the financial resources accumulated through proper stewardship.

Bringing financial order to your house isn't about having the most, or even just having more than you have now. It's about making sure that your personal financial situation can be classified as an asset and not a liability on the balance sheet of your life.

This chapter will focus on some of the most important things to know and do to bring and maintain financial order in one's house. The topics are definitely more secular than spiritual, but the purpose is to enable one to become more spiritual by being less distracted by the secular. Areas covered include debt, insurance, buying homes and cars, investments, and retirement. However, before dealing with those topics, let's tackle one with a more spiritual dimension – our own mortality.

One of the first questions I ask prospective clients is whether they have valid, up-to-date wills and powers of attorney. I'm too frequently shocked at how often couples with young children and wealthy people don't have even a basic will in place. When they don't, I make it the first order of business to get those documents in place before we proceed with any of the less pressing aspects of financial planning.

Many people procrastinate in making a will because they don't want to contemplate their death, and, in some stranger cases, believe that being prepared to die will prompt God to call them ahead of schedule. For every person who made a will and died immediately after, there are millions who died too soon and left a mess for the bereaved because there were no instructions left telling them what to do.

In the case of parents with minor children, it's essential to have a will directing who will become guardians of the children. Making this decision will involve the guardians beforehand, rather than having relatives speculate and fight over who the parents would have wanted to be the guardians of their children.

If you're a parent of a minor child and if you don't have a valid will, put making one at the top of your to-do list. You probably don't want grieving and combative relatives making that decision, and you certainly don't want your state legislature making it; they already have, by the way, in case you haven't.

Even if you have a modest estate, and especially if you have an immodest one, you need a will to keep the heirs from each other's throats after you're gone. If you don't want to do it as a courtesy to those who will most mourn your passing, do it as an opportunity to control your assets from the beyond. You can't take it with you, but you can have a say in what's done with it when you have to leave it behind.

DEBT

The tonnage of debt Americans are carrying endangers their financial health. The greater your debts, the lower your net worth, and net worth is what you live on in retirement. Debt threatens physical health because it creates stress, which weakens the immune system and makes us vulnerable to diseases like cancer and heart disease. Debt threatens mental health because it causes marital deterioration and the loss of the support system we need to survive. Debt also makes it harder to keep a proper perspective because debt can overwhelm our thoughts, making it difficult to maintain balance in our lives.

One of the more common determinants of whether a person has too much debt is the Debt-to-Income Ratio, which compares debt payments to income. Debt-to-Income Ratio is a key number lenders use to calculate a potential borrower's ability to repay any additional debt. The consensus among financial experts is that a household's debt-to-income ratio shouldn't exceed 36%.

The debt-to-income ratio is calculated by taking the total of all monthly debt payments (mortgage, home equity loan, car payments, credit cards, student loans, etc.) and dividing that total by monthly gross income. For example, a household has total gross income of $84,000, or $7,000 per month. The monthly debt payments are as follows:

• Mortgage (principal/interest/taxes/insurance)	$1,645
• Home Equity Line of Credit	$333
• Car Loan 1 (purchase)	$388
• Car Loan 2 (lease)	$249
• Credit Cards	$360
TOTAL MONTHLY DEBT SERVICE	$2,975

In this example, the debt-to-income ratio is 42.5% ($2,975/$7,000). This ratio exceeds the recommended 36%, so this household could have trouble meeting all their household expenses. The high ratio also means any additional debt may be difficult to obtain or may require higher rates of interest to offset the higher default risk.

Most of us are both borrowers <u>and</u> lenders. If you have money in the bank, you're a lender. The bank uses that money to make loans, even loans back to you. If you're both a lender and a borrower, does it make sense to pay a higher rate of interest than you receive? Of course not, but people make this mistake all the time. They may have a $5,000 CD at the bank paying 3% interest, yet they have an average balance of $2,500 on their credit cards, with an interest rate of 13%. They earn $150 interest on the CD, but pay $325 in interest on the credit card.

The disparity between interest paid and interest received isn't the only way we overpay by using debt. When we borrow to buy something, we're much more likely to pay a higher purchase price than we would if we paid cash. Numerous studies have shown that consumers will pay an average of 12-18% more for an item when they buy it on credit than when they buy the same item for cash.

Two out of five American adults have unpaid medical bills. These unpaid bills can make it harder to get needed health care; two-thirds of people with such burdens go without needed care because of the cost. That number is triple the rate of those without such financial burdens.

One of the reasons people have medical bills is health problems caused by stress about debt. It's a downward spiral for many. An AP survey compared people who reported high-debt stress with those who didn't feel such stress. In comparing the two groups, the high-debt stress group:

- Had 3½ times more ulcer/digestive problems
- Had 3 times the migraine/headache frequency
- Suffered severe anxiety at a rate 7 times higher
- Suffered severe depression at a rate 6 times higher
- Had twice as many heart attacks
- Suffered sleep disorders at a rate 13 times higher

When debts begin to pile up and just meeting the minimum monthly payments becomes a strain, the first step many people take is a debt consolidation loan. Debt consolidation is what its name implies; you take several debts and consolidate them into a single loan that should hopefully offer a lower overall interest rate than you were paying prior to consolidation.

Debt consolidation may enable a lower interest rate, but what the customer is really looking for is a lower overall monthly payment. The reason they're seeking debt consolidation in the first place is they can't handle the current size of the monthly debt service. There are three ways to reduce the size of the monthly debt service:

- Reduce the size of the overall debt, which debt consolidation doesn't do
- Reduce the interest rate, which debt consolidation might do a little
- Increase the repayment period, which debt consolidation almost always does.

The only way to get a meaningful reduction in the monthly payments is to stretch out the period of repayments.

The prospects of lower monthly payments, reducing harassing phone calls from creditors, avoiding bankruptcy, and a general easing of emotional stress are all good reasons to consider debt consolidation. However, as is the case with any financial transaction, it's important to do your homework, shop around, and read the fine print.

The easing of short-term financial pressure that debt consolidation may provide makes it even easier to continue the behaviors that created the problem in the first place. Any solution to curing a person's debt problems has to begin with behavior modification. The behavior that needs modification – spending money not yet earned.

The only program that makes sense when debt has gotten too high is to reduce that debt. The first step in reducing debt is to cancel *all* lines of credit, which means cutting up every credit card and canceling any lines of credit at banks, credit unions, etc. If you have a debt problem, you can't have access to any more credit – period. Eliminating new potential debt is the first and most crucial step in ending a credit addiction.

The fear debtors have in canceling all sources of credit is that they'll get into a position that requires the use of credit, but it won't be available. Credit is their safety net, but it's a net that ensnares, not saves. Credit isn't the solution, it's the problem, and eliminating any potential new credit is recognition of that fact.

The most successful method of knocking out debt is known as the Debt Snowball, made popular by Dave Ramsey. The Debt Snowball works in the following manner. You list your debts, smallest to largest by outstanding balance. You also list the minimum payments. The smallest debt you pay off immediately, not by borrowing, but by selling something. The main thing is to get the smallest debt off the books, without adding any additional debt.

The payments that were going toward that smallest debt are added to the payment you're making on the next smallest debt. That debt gets paid off more quickly, and the money that was paying off that debt moves to the next debt on the list. As each debt is paid off, the amount every month going to pay off the next debt on the list is increased. This process speeds up the time it takes to pay off each debt and lowers the number of outstanding debts as well. Below is a table showing an example of how the Debt Snowball works:

DEBT	INTEREST RATE	TOTAL BALANCE	MINIMUM PAYMENT	MONTHS REMAINING	NEW PAYMENT	MONTHS PAID
Target Card	16.0%	$580	$40	17	paid w/garage sale	
Sears Card	14.5%	$1,220	$85	18	$125	1-11
Discover Card	13.0%	$3,360	$120	34	$245	12-20
Visa Card	18.0%	$8,650	$245	42	$490	21-30
Home Equity	7.0%	$28,600	$360	105	$850	31-54
Student Loan	7.5%	$34,700	$366	144	$1,681	55-71
Car Loan	8.5%	$18,900	$465	48	paid off in 48 mos.	
TOTALS	8.8%avg	$96,010	$1,681			

The new payment for each debt is the minimum payment plus the sum of the payments of the debts that have been paid off. The minimum payments continue to be made for all the debts while they're waiting their turn to get an increase. In this example, the household debt of almost $100,000 is completely paid off in less than six years, they have a modest emergency fund of $2,800, and they're not only debt-free, but they can now put $1,681 a month toward building their own wealth.

Your credit score is based on your ratings in five general categories:

- Payment History (35%): shows punctuality of payments in the past
- Amounts Owed (30%): expressed as a ratio of current revolving debt to total available revolving credit
- Length of Credit History (15%): the longer the track record of paying on time, the better
- New Credit (10%): looks at new credit issued, but also at number of recent credit checks by potential lenders
- Types of Credit Used (10%): installment, revolving, consumer finance are main categories

Credit scores are being used in fields that go beyond traditional lending. Insurance companies use credit scores in underwriting risks. Potential employers look at credit scores to gauge a person's ability to handle responsibility and whether personal financial problems may create greater risk for theft or fraud.

The best methods to improve your credit score are:

- Pay your bills on time.
- If you've missed payments, get current and stay current.
- Know that paying off a collection account or closing an account doesn't remove it from your credit report.
- Contact creditors or see a legitimate credit counselor if there's a problem.
- Keep balances low on credit cards and other revolving credit.
- Pay off debt rather than moving it around.

- Avoid credit repair agencies that promise to remove negative, but accurate, information from your credit report.
- If you have a short credit history, don't open several new accounts too rapidly.
- Shop for a loan in a short period of time; it helps distinguish between a search for a single loan and a search for multiple credit lines.
- Don't open new accounts you don't need.

INSURANCE

One of great stressors is uncertainty. When you have a defense against the consequences of a bad scenario, the stress of the uncertainty goes away. Insurance takes away the uncertainty of a large loss and replaces it with the certainty of paying a relatively small premium.

Becoming disabled, even temporarily, takes a heavy toll on a person - physically, psychologically, and financially.

People don't contemplate disability insurance because they don't seriously contemplate a disability. Most disabilities are actually the result of illness, not injury.

Some statistics regarding disabilities:

- There's a one-in-three chance you'll be disabled for more than three months in your working life.
- If you're married, there's a two-in-three chance one of you will be disabled for more than three months.
- The odds of being disabled decrease with age, but only because there are fewer years to go until retirement.
- The odds of a long-term (over 90 days) disability within the next five years increase with age.

- Disabilities tend to be short or very long. If your disability lasts 90 days, it will probably last more than two years if you're young and last more than four years if you're middle-aged.

Some points to keep in mind when evaluating disability coverage:

- Think long term. A policy that covers you to age 65 is best.
- Make sure your policy is non-cancellable and has level premiums to age 65.
- Look for a waiver-of-premium provision, which waives premiums during a period of total disability.
- Look carefully at the policy's definition of disability; the broader the definition, the better.
- Not everyone is eligible for disability insurance. Pre-existing conditions are the biggest barrier.

Next to a permanent total disability, the worst financial disaster that could befall a family is the premature death of the breadwinner.

Life insurance is unique among insurance products. With almost any other type of insurance, the person paying the premium receives the benefit of the coverage. With life insurance, the person who pays the premium is typically the same person whose life is being insured. The person paying the premium is the only one who can't benefit financially from the policy.

The need for life insurance is based on the need to replace lost income for persons who depend on the insured for income. How much life insurance is needed is a function of several variables. The main goal when calculating how much life insurance is needed is to enable the beneficiaries to maintain their standard of living.

Life insurance policies can be divided into two basic types: term insurance and whole life insurance. Term life insurance provides protection for a fixed period of time, or stated term. It's the most cost-effective type of life insurance because you're buying coverage against a contingency, rather than a certainty. Whole life insurance is insurance you buy that will last your whole life, as will the premiums. Whole life insurance is needed when you'll have outstanding financial obligations whenever you die.

Whole life insurance is considerably more expensive than term insurance because as long as the premiums are paid, the death benefit will also be paid. Also, the premiums on a whole life insurance policy remain level from day one.

Health care and health insurance are important issues because everyone needs to attend to their health, and everyone, with the exception of the extremely wealthy, needs health insurance to assure getting proper medical care in a crisis.

Medical care expenses can be broken down into three categories:

- Ordinary medical expenses: those considered routine
- Extraordinary medical expenses: go beyond the routine, but are not uncommon
- Catastrophic medical expenses: those resulting from catastrophic illness or injury

Many health insurance policies give you options. When choosing which option is best for you and your family, premiums will play a part in that decision, but look carefully at the benefits offered by the different options, including deductibles, co-pays, and the percentage the plan pays.

Of all the health care expenses we'll incur over our lifetime, half of them will be incurred in the last five years of our lives. Part of that imbalance can be blamed on inflation, but most of it is the result of needing more intensive and more expensive care as we age.

Living in a decent nursing home can run over $100,000 per year, and Medicare doesn't cover long-term care. Medicaid provides for long-term care, but almost exclusively to the aged, blind, and disabled group of eligible beneficiaries. Currently, about 60% of the population over age 65 will need some type of long-term care over their lifetime.

Once you turn fifty, it's time to start looking at long-term care insurance. If you wait too long, you may develop a medical condition that makes long-term care insurance far more expensive, or even unattainable.

The costs associated with long-term care do more to damage the financial stability of seniors (not to mention consuming inheritances) than anything else, which is reason enough to investigate long-term care insurance.

For most of us, our single most valuable possession is our home, and we naturally need to protect ourselves from loss related to that asset. Homeowners' insurance is a package policy that combines all the needed types of coverage into one policy:

- The dwelling itself
- Other structures detached from the main dwelling
- Personal property, at home or away
- Loss of use of your home from a covered incident
- Liability coverage and legal defense

Homeowners' insurance is required if you have a mortgage, but it's necessary for anyone who owns a home or condo. For what it covers, it's one of the best bargains in insurance. Even if you rent, you need Renters' insurance for all the same reasons.

One of the first things to understand about auto insurance is that the insurance is first on the car and then on the driver. On an auto insurance policy, specific vehicles are listed.

The states require that you have liability coverage to protect others in the event you cause an accident. Other coverages are optional, although, if you have a loan on a car, the lender will require comprehensive and collision coverages. States set minimum liability limits.

There's a coverage called uninsured/underinsured motorist coverage. If you're involved in an accident that isn't your fault and if the other driver has no insurance or inadequate insurance, your uninsured/underinsured motorist coverage will pay you for your medical bills, property damage, and pain and suffering. It's not mandatory, but highly recommended.

There are two types of coverage for damage to your own auto. Collision coverage is used when your vehicle hits or is hit by another car or when your car hits something stationary, like a building. Comprehensive coverage covers things like fire, theft, hail damage, flood, and being attacked by a deer.

BUYING HOMES AND CARS

Before you begin looking at potential houses to buy, it's important to do some preliminary work. First, determine how much house you can afford to buy and arrange financing for that amount.

The first step in arranging financing is to get a copy of your credit report and credit score to confirm all the information is accurate and up-to-date. Check your credit report three months before seeking financing. If there are errors that lower your credit score (there's a 25% chance), allow time to get the errors corrected before you attempt to get financing.

Assuming your credit report is complete and accurate, comparison shop for mortgages. Consider only fixed-rate mortgages. Adjustable-rate mortgages may look tempting because the initial interest rate is lower than a fixed-rate mortgage. However, the borrower assumes the risk of rising interest rates. You may end up with a mortgage payment that becomes unmanageable if the lender has the ability to move your interest rate when rates climb.

If you can find the home you want and finance it with a 15-year mortgage, by all means do so. Everything else being equal, a 15-year mortgage usually has an interest rate about ¼ point less than a 30-year mortgage.

MONTHLY MORTGAGE PAYMENTS FOR EACH $50,000 BORROWED AT VARIOUS INTEREST RATES*

Interest Rate	15-Year Mortgage	Total Repayment	30-Year Mortgage	Total Repayment
4.00%	$369.84	$66,571.20	$238.71	$85,935.60
4.25%	$376.14	$67,705.20	$245.97	$88,549.20
4.50%	$382.50	$68,850.00	$253.34	$91,204.40
4.75%	$388.92	$70,005.60	$260.82	$93,895.20
5.00%	$395.40	$71,172.00	$268.41	$96,627.60
5.25%	$401.94	$72,349.20	$276.10	$99,396.00
5.50%	$408.54	$73,537.20	$283.89	$102,200.40
5.75%	$415.21	$74,737.80	$291.79	$105,044.40
6.00%	$421.93	$75,947.40	$299.78	$107,920.80
6.25%	$428.71	$77,167.80	$307.86	$110,829.60
6.50%	$435.55	$78,399.00	$316.03	$113,770.80
6.75%	$442.45	$79,641.00	$324.30	$116,748.00
7.00%	$449.41	$80,893.80	$332.65	$119.754.00
7.25%	$456.43	$82,157.40	$341.09	$122,792.40
7.50%	$463.51	$83,431.80	$349.61	$125,859.60
7.75%	$470.64	$84,715.20	$358.21	$128,955.60

*Mortgage payments include principal and interest, but don't include property taxes or insurance.

Use a realtor. This advice applies whether you're buying or selling a home. If you're buying a home, bringing in a realtor as your agent can help you avoid costly mistakes, especially if you're new to the process or to the area. If you're selling a home, a realtor will bring more potential buyers, will likely get a higher price to at least offset the commission, and will help you avoid mistakes that may cost thousands of dollars while potentially creating a legal mess.

Here are some specifics to consider when evaluating a house and the neighborhood:

- *Location on the street* – Cul-de-sacs are quieter than the middle of a long straightaway on a through street.
- *Adjoining properties* – Being surrounded by similar homes offers protection against unwanted change.
- *Rented homes nearby* – A neighborhood with a lot of rental houses is usually in a downward transition.
- *Relativity* – A house that's different in price or style from nearby houses may be difficult to sell.
- *Terrain* – A lot that slopes may be prone to flooding or hard to traverse in bad weather.
- *Homeowners Association* – Learn what the annual dues are and what the restrictions are, too.
- *Corner lots* – There's more traffic and it's difficult to configure the back yard to provide privacy.
- *Bedrooms and baths* - Fewer than three bedrooms and one-and-a-half baths may limit resale potential.
- *Waterfront property* – You pay for a view, but also get boat traffic and less privacy.
- *Mountain property* – You pay for a view, but are often isolated and hard to access in bad weather.
- *HVAC units* – Separate heating/cooling units for each floor will be more energy efficient.

- *Septic or sewage* – Public sewage has higher monthly cost, but malfunctioning septic can be a nightmare.
- *Condition* – Getting a deal on a poorly maintained house rarely ends up being a deal in the long run.
- *Convenience* – Notice the proximity to shopping, hospitals, fire, and police stations.
- *Landscaping* – The appearance may not be worth the time and expense to keep up appearances.
- *Trees* – Mature trees add to the beauty of the property, but they're a potential risk if they fall.
- *Updates* – Some items are just trendy, and don't add value over the long-term.
- *Age of mechanicals* – Inspect HVAC units, appliances, water heaters, or anything with moving parts.
- *Age of roof* – Have the roof inspected and get an estimate of remaining life.
- *Water spots* – These indicate water leakage, and the source needs to be found and fixed.
- *Energy bills* – Ask to see the seller's utility bills over the last twelve months, so you know what to expect.
- *Property taxes* – Taxes are nearly as important as the selling price in determining affordability.

There's no practical reason for much of the extra spending Americans do when it comes to cars. Lincolns and Lexuses have more status (we assume) than Fords and Toyotas, and we're willing to pay a lot for that status. We pay, on average, the cost of a year's tuition at a public university for nothing more than the opportunity to feel superior to those with "inferior" rides. It's troubling that there are millions of Americans driving a status symbol who aren't saving enough for retirement.

Every car you consider must fit your needs (not your desires) and your budget. Fitting your budget is a function of the car's price; everything else is a product of that number, so that's the number that requires a firm limit. The most important thing you can do to get the right car at the right price is research before you look at cars. A couple of hours on the internet can save thousands of dollars.

Internet research gives you the opportunity to collect data on several different models of cars. You can do side-by-side comparisons and access road test reviews and consumer ratings for cars that interest you.

You can also research financing options on line. First, find out your current credit score, as it will affect financing options. You can look up current rates on different financing packages, and even get pre-qualified for a loan.

The best feature of internet research is that you're doing it on your turf and on your terms. When you're at the car dealer, you're on their turf and are largely under their control. When trying to determine the best car for your needs, you don't need aggressive sales people or even the allure of the car itself to distract you.

Consider models from more than one manufacturer, which can improve leverage in negotiations. Let the dealers know you're considering other models from other manufacturers

Learning about the cars you're considering will help you by demonstrating you've done your research. You'll be sized up as a savvy consumer, and you're more likely to be treated with the respect you deserve.

Leasing can make sense under these conditions:

- You're getting a sensible car you could afford to buy.

- You're saving/investing the difference between the lease payment and the purchase payment.
- You're unlikely to drive over the mileage limit, but likely to drive close to the mileage limit.
- You'll be maintaining the car properly.
- You negotiated your lease deal, just like a purchase.
- You won't have to change cars during the lease period (i.e. – Sports cars and infants don't mix.)

For most people, the second largest cost of a car, after the monthly payment, is the insurance premium. For some, it can even exceed the monthly payment. An unexpectedly high insurance premium may force you into selling the car shortly after buying it. If it's a leased vehicle, you may be stuck until the end of the lease period.

It's important to shop for car insurance in concert with shopping for the car itself. Often, the cheaper car to purchase isn't the cheaper car to own, when other costs, especially insurance, are factored in.

INVESTMENTS

There's no magic formula to creating wealth. Work. Earn. Invest. Repeat. That's all. It's not complicated, merely hard, which is why so few people are wealthy. Most people are willing to do the work. Most people aren't willing to do the delayed gratification. Delayed gratification requires discipline and a long-term perspective.

Just as work is an essential ingredient to creating wealth, work is also an essential ingredient to anything claiming to be an investment. Simply put, an investment does work. The more work it does, the more it will earn. Like people, an investment can only do so much work at a time. A true investment makes you rich over time, but not overnight.

The only number that really matters when judging the performance of an investment is total return. Total return includes any interest or dividends an investment yields, plus capital gains and unrealized appreciation in the investment's market value. Total return gives the truest picture of how an investment is performing.

There's actually a system to get superior returns with almost no effort. It's called dollar-cost averaging. Here's how this system works. Take a percentage of your income this month and invest it in something like the S&P 500. Do the same thing next month and the next month and the month after that. Keep doing it as long as you're earning an income. Then stop and see how much you've got. That's it.

It's possible you're already using this method without realizing it. If you're investing money into your 401k every month and if you put the same amount every month into the same investments, you're doing dollar-cost averaging.

Here's why dollar-cost averaging is such a good system. If you put $100 a month into a mutual fund and if the share price that month is $25, you'll buy four shares. If the share price the next month drops to $20, you'll buy 5 shares. You automatically buy more shares when the price is lower and fewer shares when the price is higher. This system enables you to buy shares for an average lower price, which will give you superior returns to the actual investment. And it requires nothing more than setting it up and funding it.

A *bond* is simply an IOU that's issued by a corporation or government entity. When you buy a bond, you're lending the money to the bond issuer.

Bonds, as a whole, have lower volatility than stocks. Bonds, as a whole, also have lower long-term returns than stocks. Since stocks involve a greater risk, they should provide a greater return than bonds over the long term.

If you're bondholder, you get paid before the stockholders do. Bondholders get their money first, but they never get more than what the bond agreement states. Stockholders aren't assured of anything, but they get everything that's left after the company's obligations are met.

Bonds are favored by those who favor stability and modest growth over larger returns. Trusts, endowment funds, and insurance companies have large bond holdings because a modest return is preferable to a large potential loss.

Bond returns over the last eighty years have averaged 5-6% per year. Inflation over this same period has averaged just over 3% per year. Interest rates are a function of inflation. When inflation is higher, interest rates must also be higher to induce people to save rather than spend. Bond returns have historically been 2-3% above inflation.

When you own bonds, you've chosen greater security over greater opportunity. That's the appropriate choice regarding any money that you'll be spending within the next five years. In the short term, the return *of* the money is more important than the return *on* the money.

Saving is what you do for the short term. Investing is what you do for the long term. When you invest money that won't be spent for decades to come, you want to invest in a way that gives you the best long-term returns. As long-term investments go, stocks are hard to beat.

The wealthiest people you know personally are probably owners of their own businesses, or stockholders in companies. When you're a stockholder, you own a piece of the company. You're like Bill Gates or Warren Buffett, albeit on a smaller scale.

In the short term, the stock market is a voting mechanism, reflecting our expectations of profits. In the long term, the stock market is a weighing mechanism, reflecting the actual profits. The history of actual profits is a fairly smooth, fairly continuous upsloping line. Our expectations of profits are constantly buffeted by greed and fear, by good news and bad news, by taking the recent past and extrapolating it out into the indefinite future.

If the prospect of selecting and monitoring a portfolio of individual stocks intimidates you, then using mutual funds as your primary investment vehicles may make more sense.

A mutual fund is simply a collection of stocks, bonds, or other securities that are purchased by a group of investors and managed by an investment company. When you buy a share of a mutual fund, you're buying a piece of the entire portfolio of that mutual fund.

Here are the most important features of mutual funds:

- *Diversification* – When you own shares of a mutual fund, you own a piece of every asset owned by the mutual fund. Mutual funds enable smaller investors to get a properly diversified portfolio.
- *Asset Allocation* – If you should have a portfolio consisting of 25% bonds and 75% stocks, you can buy individual mutual funds to create that allocation, or you can buy a single mutual fund with that allocation.
- *Liquidity* – Open-ended mutual funds (which most

funds are) are required to buy back the shares from shareholders at market price upon demand.

- *Professional Management* – Along with diversification, professional management is probably the best feature of the mutual fund. By directing others to look after the day-to-day oversight of your portfolio, you're freed from having to do it.

The prospect of outliving their money is one of the worst scenarios most retirees can imagine. It isn't just the financial strain; the loss of independence and dignity associated with having to ask relatives or agencies for assistance is a psychological strain, too. With the disappearance of traditional pensions, the prospect of outliving your money is more common now. There is a financial product that replaces the traditional pension – the annuity.

Both life insurance and annuities protect against the loss of income. Life insurance assures income if you die too soon. Annuities assure income if you live too long.

The most important feature of an annuity is the promise to pay a lifetime income to the annuitant, regardless of how long that person lives. Traditional pensions were an annuity in the sense that they made the same promise to pay as long as the retiree or spouse were living.

An annuity works this way. You pay premiums to the annuity company. There's no set amount or timetable. That money grows in your account. When you're ready to begin your annuity, a calculation is made for a regular income based on the value of your account and your life expectancy from mortality tables. They pay you the same amount at the same interval as long as you're drawing breaths. The possibility of outliving your income has been eliminated, which is the most reassuring aspect of the annuity.

A *fixed annuity* is one that pays a fixed rate of return for the period the money is in the account. The rate of return may be adjusted periodically, but it can never go below a certain amount. *Variable annuities* allow the owner of the annuity to invest in mutual funds within the annuity. The owner can choose the level of aggressiveness. There's no minimum guaranteed return with a variable annuity; there's also no maximum return.

RETIREMENT

In 1935, when The Social Security Act was signed into law, the selected retirement age was set at 65, in part because only half of the nation's workers lived that long. Those workers who made it to age 65 collected Social Security for only five years on average before they died. They basically worked ten years for each year spent in retirement.

Today, college graduates start work around age 22. Their goal typically is to retire at age 62, currently the earliest age to collect Social Security retirement benefits. A 62-year-old today can expect to live 23 more years, on average. Forty years from now, when that 22-year-old is 62, he/she can expect about 30 more years of life.

On the day today's graduates begin full-time work, they have 70 years of life left. They plan to only work the first 40 years, then live off their accumulated savings for the last 30 years. It's a huge change from when people worked 50 years with the hope they could retire for the last 5 years. The ratio of work to retirement has gone from 50:5 to 40:30.

In most corporations, the defined benefit retirement plan has been replaced by the defined contribution retirement plan. The employer defines the *contribution* they'll make each year to an employee's retirement account, rather than defining the *benefit* the employee will receive at retirement. The contribution calculation typically involves a percentage of the employee's salary, and/or a contribution based on the company's profitability. An even more important difference is that, while most, if not all, of the cost of funding a defined benefit plan was paid by the employer, most, if not all, of the cost of a defined contribution plan is paid by the employee through participation in plans like 401(k)s.

With this change, the safety net of a guaranteed income at retirement is gone. The employer meets its obligation to your retirement funding during your employment, not during your retirement.

Almost every calculation I make indicates people should be saving *at least* 10% of their income for retirement. Even a brand new college graduate, with forty-five years of work ahead, should be saving 10% of every paycheck in order to retire properly around sixty-seven. Delays in starting and not saving enough early on can raise the required saving rate considerably in middle age.

Historically, people have been told that they would need approximately 75% of their pre-retirement income in retirement to continue the same standard of living. This is a generic number, but it serves as a starting point. The actual retirement income will, of course, be a function of how much a person saved prior to retirement.

Calculating the necessary size of your retirement fund when you begin retirement requires you to consider the following:

- The level of income you'll need in retirement compared to your income just before retirement

- Your income and spending levels in those last few years of work
- How long you'll be retired (The earlier you retire, the longer the retirement.)

Twenty times - when asked how much money someone needs to save for retirement, a standard answer is twenty times the required income in the first year of retirement. The second part of the standard answer is that you'll annually draw 5% of the value of the investments as income in the first years of retirement.

Inflation will make the last thirty years of your life your most expensive. Even if you reduce your expenses going into retirement, inflation will soon have your expenses back to their old level, and they'll keep increasing.

Inflation is the most misunderstood and the most insidious enemy of retirees. Inflation is simply a decline in purchasing power as a result of rising prices. Retirees often have little discretionary income. They also often have little, if any, ability to increase their income in retirement.

The goal of a retirement portfolio is to provide returns that will enable you to stay ahead of inflation, while at the same time smoothing out volatility as much as possible, which is the purpose of diversification. If your money is spread out over not just several assets, but several different asset classes, you're much more likely to get returns that will enable you to maintain your standard of living and to also keep the portfolio from having the kind of down years from which recovery is difficult.

Diversification means you have positions in large U.S. companies, small growing U.S. companies, established overseas companies and developing overseas companies. You also have some bond holdings and some cash in money market funds. Your asset/income ratio, as well as your personal tolerance for risk and volatility, will be large factors in the actual asset allocation. The following are general recommendations.

First, whatever amount you plan to draw from the retirement account over the next 18-24 months should be in nothing riskier than a money market fund. Even if that money market fund is paying a low interest rate, you need to know that the value won't drop. When you're looking at having to use that money to pay a bill within a year or two, it's the return *of* the money, not the return *on* the money that's of greatest importance.

Next, whatever amount you plan to draw from the account over four to five more years should be in short-term and intermediate-term high quality bonds/bond funds. These bonds tend to pay a better interest rate than money market funds, with lower volatility than stocks.

By having five to six years of income in something other than stocks, you're able to ride out the worst bear markets. By having six years' income in bonds and cash, there would be no need to sell a stock holding when it's down due to a bear market. You have a cushion of time to enable that part of your portfolio to recover.

The remainder of your investment portfolio is going to do the long-term heavy lifting, which is the 2/3 to 3/4 that will be devoted to stocks. Only stocks have shown the ability to generate long-term returns that will keep the portfolio growing well ahead of the inflation rate. While stocks may comprise 2/3 to 3/4 of your portfolio, they'll be responsible for 90% or more of the income and appreciation generated by the portfolio.

As a very general guide, retirees should have at least 50% of their stock holdings invested in large U.S. companies, the kind of companies that you find in the S&P 500 and similar large company indexes. These companies offer stability, as well as historically good returns. They may fluctuate in value, but they rarely go out of business.

The remainder of a retiree's stock holdings should be divided between small U.S. companies, large foreign companies, and developing markets. The small U.S. companies are small only in comparison to the Fortune 500 companies. Many companies with a market value of $5 billion are classified as small companies. These companies are typically on the cutting edge of new markets and technologies.

Large foreign companies offer stability and the opportunity to diversify beyond the U.S. economy. Many of these companies are familiar to Americans. They include names like Toyota, Nestle, BP, and Samsung. These companies are less affected by adverse economic conditions in the U.S. than companies that are strictly domestic.

Lastly, developing markets offer excellent long-term growth potential, countries like Hungary, Thailand, and India. We're referring to countries with established infrastructures, representative governments, and transparent accounting.

Each year, money for income will come out of the money market fund. When it comes time to replacing that money each year, the investment categories that have done the best in the previous year will be sold down to provide the cash. In most years, creating cash for income will mean selling some of the various stock holdings. This strategy does two things – it disciplines you to sell when the asset is high, and it rebalances the portfolio at the same time.

Financial stability in your own house is created through the proper use of wills, insurance, investments, retirement accounts, as well as the careful acquisition of major purchases like homes and cars. Creating financial stability in your own house enables you to help create financial stability in other houses, especially God's.

FINANCIAL STABILITY IN GOD'S HOUSE

Are you a renter or an owner? I'm not referring here to your home or your car; I'm referring to your place of worship.

To determine the answer to that question, see how you answer the following questions:

- Do you value your membership on an *absolute* basis or a *relative* basis? In other words, how much of the value of your membership is set by you, and how much is based on how others perceive that value, or how you value it compared to the alternatives?
- Does your offering in the collection plate feel more like an investment or more like membership dues?
- Which do you spend more time discussing with non-members, your church's successes or its failures?
- Do you set strict limits on the time, talent, and treasure you'll contribute?
- When a situation requires additional resources, do you wait until someone makes a personal request before responding?

- When change occurs and you don't like it, is leaving one of the first options you consider?
- Do you view a solicitation to give time, talent, or treasure as an opportunity or an imposition?
- When something isn't going right, do you look for who's responsible first?
- Does your circle of friends include church members in proportion to the universe of people you know?
- Is your participation limited to one morning per week, at most?
- How many of the staff know you by name?
- Do you know, within roughly 10%, the annual income and expenses of your church?

There are no right or wrong answers to these questions, but how you truthfully answer them can give a strong indication of whether you're an owner or a renter where you worship.

As a basis of comparison, think about how you would answer questions like these regarding other things in your life – your home, your car, your family, your employer, your community, or other organizations or groups with which you associate.

To be an owner means to have a stake in something – an equity stake. If you own your home, you take responsibility for its upkeep because you're the one most affected by how well your home is maintained. The same is true of all your possessions. You care for your family, your community, your employer, and any group you join because their fates are linked with yours. To be a good steward in these situations is easy because there's a high level of self-interest.

In writing about the Middle East in 2002, journalist Thomas Friedman cited a perspective espoused by others: "In the entire history of the world, no one ever washed a rented car." While perhaps not technically correct, the meaning is clear. When we feel no sense of ownership, we feel far less obligation to care for something. In his reference to the Middle East, Friedman was saying that people in many of those countries feel no sense of ownership of their countries. The dictators control everything, and the people perceive nothing to be gained in making improvements.

The difference between an owner and a renter isn't merely one of legal ownership. The difference is, more than anything, a difference in the level of commitment. It's the difference between marriage and dating, between volunteering and being drafted, between "ought to" and "want to".

In a place of worship, the 80/20 principle manifests itself whereby 20% of the members give 80% of the time, talent, and treasure. Whatever this ratio is for a particular organization, it's also a measure of the renter/owner ratio. If 20% of the people at your church do 80% of everything, those 20% are the owners of your church; everyone else is a renter.

Those who think it's smarter to be a renter and not have to do a disproportionate amount of giving forget the most important aspect of the 80/20 principle at work here – the 20% doing the work and the giving are also receiving *at least* 80% of the benefits of membership.

The benefits these owners receive are like water that comes from an old-fashioned hand pump. Before you can get water flowing from the spout, you first have to prime the pump, which means pumping away to get the water to rise from the underground well to the surface. The deeper the water source, the more priming of the pump is needed.

Renters are like those people who are thirsty, who go to the pump, pump the handle a few times, and then walk away still thirsty because no water came out immediately. Owners are like those people who know two things: there's water down there, and they're thirsty and want some. They'll keep pumping that handle until the water comes gushing forth. Their motto is simple – *whatever it takes*.

When a house of worship is struggling financially, it's almost always a symptom of a lack of ownership by the members. Too many are only willing to rent pew space on a week-to-week basis, and there are too few willing to invest in an equity stake in that house.

The real estate crisis of the past few years has had one common thread running through it. This common thread crossed all geographic, economic, social, racial, religious lines and has been confirmed with numerous studies. The common thread was: the smaller the down payment, as a percentage of the purchase price, the greater the default rate on the mortgage.

People who made a substantial down payment had more "skin in the game". They not only made a greater effort to maintain their mortgages, they also made a greater effort to maintain their homes, and their properties reflect their greater commitment.

Whatever touches our hearts tends to touch our wallets as well. It's one reason why commercials for well-meaning organizations show pictures of sad and deprived puppies or children. These organizations have a mission to help these puppies or children, and they know the money follows the mission.

Where our hearts are, our treasures follow. While this is a true statement, it's the opposite of what Jesus taught. Jesus said, "Where your treasure is, there your heart will be also." However, Jesus is not merely making a statement of fact. The full text of Luke, Chapter 12: 32-34 is:

> *"Do not be afraid, little flock, for your Father has been pleased to give you the Kingdom. Sell your possessions and give to the poor. Provide purses for yourselves that will not wear out, a treasure in heaven that will not be exhausted, where no thief comes near and no moth destroys. For where your treasure is, there your heart will be also."*

What Jesus is also saying is, *where you want your heart to be*, put your treasure there first, and your heart will follow it. Going back to the 80/20 principle, 80% of the members are waiting to feel the call of the heart before they contribute their treasure. The other 20% understand that contributing their treasure to where they want their hearts to be brings their hearts to that place, just as Jesus said. In most places of worship, 20% get it; 80% don't.

The goal of every house of worship should be to make every member become an owner, not just a renter. A sense of ownership breeds loyalty, commitment, a sense of mission, and a true feeling of belonging, which is something almost everyone is seeking in their religious life.

It may seem cold to say, but if someone doesn't think they can *ever* feel like an owner in their church, it's time to find another church. If they can't bring themselves to commit the time, talent, and treasure to bring their heart fully into their house of worship and if they believe that doing so still won't bring their heart into that place, they need to seek out a place where that change can happen.

Let me extend a note of caution, though. Every religious institution, every denomination has its flaws. If someone is looking for the perfect fit, whether in a partner or a parish, they'll only be disappointed in the end. Places of worship have the same flaws as other organizations and institutions because there are humans involved in all of them.

Time, talent, and treasure are the Trinity of Gifts – we've been given all three and are expected to give all three as we've been given. All three are unique in what they offer to the giver and to the receiver.

Time is the most equally distributed gift from God. Everyone gets the same number of minutes every day. Time is a gift we often use unwisely, though. Even at church, too much time is often wasted at meetings that don't accomplish anything. However, when someone simply needs to have another person spend some time with them, time becomes the most irreplaceable and precious of gifts.

Among the Trinity of Gifts, talent is probably the one we're most willing to give, in part because our supply of talent doesn't diminish when we give it, and we also like the ego boost we get when we display our talents. The challenge in most groups like churches is finding out the talents of the members and utilizing those talents to their fullest extent.

The giving of time and talent is essential for any house of worship for several reasons. The receiving of these gifts enables the church to fulfill its missions. Time and talent not given by members may have to be purchased on the open market, requiring more treasure to do so. The giving of these gifts creates ownership on the part of the givers in a way that giving treasure alone doesn't. For example, if the church has a "Campus

Beautification Day", those people who show up to plant flowers, pull weeds, and spread mulch receive more joy and create a greater sense of ownership than someone who simply writes a check to pay for the flowers and mulch.

All three gifts are essential for the well-being of the giver and the receiver. Giving treasure alone is a poor substitute for giving time and talent. However, there are many, many circumstances where time and talent, no matter how great the quantities, are simply no substitute for treasure.

For better or worse, money is our primary method of contact with the secular world. Outside of family and close friends, most of our contact with other people has a monetary component, which is in large part because money performs so many different functions.

Every house of worship has interactions with the secular world. Here are just a few of the ways money is the only gift that works:

- All staff, including clergy, need to be paid in money because they all have households to run that require money to run them.
- Insurance on people and property requires the payment of premiums, which is just another term for money.
- Utility companies send monthly bills that require prompt payment, in money.
- Office operations require equipment and supplies that have to be purchased or leased, with money.
- Maintenance and repairs that are beyond the ability of members to do require hiring outside professionals.
- Large building projects typically require outside financing, creating a mortgage payable in money only.

- Transportation, travel, conferences, etc. for clergy and staff all require money.
- Education and outreach programs, while supported largely with time and talent, require money to some degree to operate.
- In my Episcopal Church, we have an annual Diocesan assessment of approximately 10% of our operating revenues. Even within our own denomination, money is the only legal tender to meet certain obligations.

When it comes to giving money, it's far easier for people to give to specific causes they strongly support. Some people love music and give to the music program. Some people feel outreach is the main mission of their church and write checks to support that cause. Rarely does anyone write a check to support keeping the lights on (unless the lights have been recently turned off due to non-payment).

The church's operating budget consists of all the areas that require money to function. Even if areas like music and outreach have a large time and talent component, there's still an essential treasure component that has to be met.

Most items in the operating budget don't elicit the kind of emotional response that prompts people to designate funds for that item. However, because these more mundane areas are nevertheless essential for a church to function, it's critical that the great majority of the treasure given to the church be non-designated funds; in other words, funds to cover the operational budget of the church, as directed by the church leadership.

One sign that a church is in trouble is what I call the *balkanization of giving*. When people don't trust those responsible for the finances of the church or when they feel that their favorite programs are inadequately funded, they reduce their giving to the operating budget and convert those funds into designated gifts.

Even though total giving may not decline as a result of this balkanization of giving, when everyone takes ownership of only a small piece of the church, no one takes ownership of the church as a whole. The membership subdivides themselves into smaller and smaller Balkan-like states, the church equivalent of Yugoslavia breaking into seven different countries, often with similar levels of animosity toward each other.

While there's certainly nothing wrong in supporting programs that are important to you, it should never come at the expense of the overall financial health of the church. Once your proportionate responsibility toward the church's operating budget has been met, I encourage you to give generously to the specific programs that mean the most to you. Specific support should always be *in addition to, not instead of*, general support.

Some people use money to send a message at their house of worship. That message is sent more often by withholding funding, rather than by designating funding. If they think the pastor is overpaid, they give less overall and designate a large portion to specific programs. They seek to effect change by controlling the flow of funds.

That strategy may be effective in business, but a church isn't a business; it's your spiritual family. And you don't punish family by withholding necessary financial support. Before using money in such a manner, it's necessary to recognize that money is the primary tool adults use to bully each other.

Too often, when things don't go our way at our church, we start shopping around for a new church. We may justify leaving with claims like, "I'm not being fed." or, "They're not biblical enough." Often, the real, unspoken reason is something less spiritual, like, "The sermons are too long." or "They spend too much on youth programs."

In his book, *Death by Suburb – How to Keep the Suburbs from Killing Your Soul*, David L. Goetz devotes a chapter to why you should stay at your church, especially when it's tempting to leave:

- Freedom often means staying, not leaving. Like in marriage, staying gives God the opportunity to show you "the thicker life".
- Bouncing from church to church can become less like shopping and more like casual sex.
- The real journey to God involves, at least in part, the relationships of the worshipping community.
- The more "knowledgeable" one is on religious teachings, the more apt he or she is to be cynical about the flaws in the church.
- It's always easier to leave than to go deep.
- We learn about the Christian virtues of acceptance and graciousness, even when we're not accepting and gracious.
- Staying put is a spiritual discipline that allows God's grace to work on the unsanded surfaces of your inner life.

One's church can be a lot like one's spouse. They're not perfect, but one should never expect them to be. They require constant assistance to meet expectations, and even then they may disappoint. Others may be more influential, and they rarely seem to be on the same side as you. They could be better with money. They could be less annoying. They could be more supportive. They could, if only they would try, be better than they are now.

All of these things, and more, can be true if we think that our church (or our spouse) exists to meet our needs. God calls us to serve, not to be served. If we expect a spouse or a church to focus on meeting our needs, rather than our focusing on meeting their needs, we'll spend our lives in a fruitless search for the right church or the right spouse.

Most places of worship that have financial difficulties fail to do two things. First, they fail to talk openly and honestly about money. As a result of the first, and more important, they fail to cultivate a culture of generosity.

Generosity begins with the understanding and acceptance that we are but stewards, and when we give, we're merely passing on to others what God has passed on to us. As governments are constantly proving, it's easy to be generous with others' money. By recognizing that all we have, including our money, isn't really ours, but God's, it becomes a whole lot easier to give it away, even cheerfully as God wants. Generosity is the fullest expression of stewardship.

Generosity is contagious, far more contagious than its opposite, stinginess. While many may be stingy, no one honestly likes the way it makes them feel. True generosity gives a buzz that can be quite addictive.

A church that cultivates a generosity mindset in its members is also a church that's generous to its members and to the secular world. Generosity is one of the key ingredients necessary for any house of God to fulfill its mission.

During the Great Recession of recent times, many churches demonstrated a culture of scarcity, instead of a culture of generosity, by reducing spending and cutting back on all "non-essential" expenditures. Most of those non-essential expenditures involved helping the less fortunate, especially those outside the church. The message the church leadership sent to the congregation was clear – we're a culture of scarcity, not generosity.

Culture is shaped by intentional, systematic processes, not by the occasional sermon during the stewardship campaign. The culture has to encourage generosity, celebrate it, and reproduce it through a process over time.

The goal in creating a culture of generosity is NOT to raise money. A larger church budget may be one effect of a new culture of generosity, but it must always be an effect, a happy unintended consequence; it must never be the cause.

If church leaders don't value generosity and practice it, they can't expect the people in the church to do so, either. In order to change people from consumers to givers, leaders need to have candid conversations about money. By explicitly letting others know by word and deed that generosity is one of the core values of a church, the leaders will create a culture of generosity in their church – not overnight, but over time.

A culture of generosity is about raising souls, not about raising money. One of the best measures of how deep the culture of generosity is forming is how much members are giving to worthy causes *outside* the church. A so-called culture of generosity that only manifests itself within the church walls isn't a culture; it's fund-raising.

As proof that a church wants to develop a culture of generosity and not just raise funds, church leaders should encourage giving to outside causes with no direct connection to the church. An effective statement to that effect might go something like this:

"God wants you to experience the joy that comes from giving from the heart, not from any compulsion. To that end, we would like everyone to increase their giving by 10% over the next year, but we want all of the increase to go to some cause *other* than this place of worship. We want you to become more generous for your sake, not for ours."

The inevitable result of such an approach over time will be an increase in giving to outside causes *and* to the church. There's no way that, over time, the place that fosters a culture of generosity won't become one of its major beneficiaries. It has to come as the effect, though, not the cause.

A successful strategy for creating a culture of generosity involves information, application, and transformation.

Information begins with educating on what is meant by generosity and stewardship. At a minimum, this part of the process should serve to alleviate suspicions that the whole process is nothing more than fund-raising in a different wrapper.

Application begins by setting expectations. People need to know specifically what they're expected to do; when they don't know, they're almost always going to do less. Clear expectations also enable the person to feel good about what they've done when they meet or exceed expectations.

Transformation can't be controlled, and it begins subtly. Evidence of individual transformation will come slowly and unevenly. Evidence of transformation at the level of church leadership will do a lot to spur transformation at the individual level.

A culture of generosity doesn't always mesh with a conservative approach to finance. There's a certain sense of recklessness that trusts God to take care of us if we take care of others, though God's track record in this area should offer no small reassurance.

A culture of generosity is not the same as giving-in-order-to-receive. While God has historically been very generous to those who are good stewards and are generous themselves, whenever the goal of giving is to receive more, we simply put a mask of generosity on the face of selfishness. True generosity is anonymous, unrequited giving with no expectations and no strings attached.

If money is the most powerful secular force on earth and if it has the potential to be a source of great good as well as great harm, why are church leaders so afraid to speak about it openly, passionately, and frequently? Too often, church leaders interpret a desire by the congregation to not be asked for money all the time as a desire not to talk about money at all. In fact, if church leaders would talk (not ask) about money more often, the resistance to being asked for money would largely fade away.

The message could begin with something as simple as this – "Generosity is something God wants *for* you, not *from* you." Creating a culture of generosity should be done for selfless, not selfish reasons. Church leaders should emphasize that becoming a generous person, even if that generosity does nothing to improve church finances, is something they want for everyone. They can even encourage the first act of greater generosity be directed at something other than the church.

Generosity is an act that nurtures the soul of the giver and the receiver. The goal in creating a culture of generosity is to change lives. Generous giving frees the giver from attachment to material things.

In another of my books, *Whipsawed – How Greed and Fear Shred Finances and Futures*, I recommend that the antidote to financial fear is saving, and the antidote to all kinds of greed is giving. Brain studies have even shown that there are two distinct parts of the brain that control our greed and generosity, and those parts cannot function simultaneously. Greed immobilizes generosity, but generosity also immobilizes greed.

People want direction, but they also need to feel empowered. Too often, those in leadership positions lay out a plan and then solicit the help of the congregation. Everyone has an idea of what they want to accomplish in the name of God, and far more could be accomplished if the church and its leaders could provide guidance and assistance in helping individuals to do God's will as they see it, not just as a few in leadership positions see it.

Those people with large incomes and/or wealth may need to develop a generous spirit, even more than those with more modest means. Jesus talks about how difficult it is for the wealthy to enter the Kingdom of God. Those of means need to learn how they can grow spiritually and also be reassured that they won't be spiritually spurned just because they've experienced secular success.

High-capacity givers are more likely to respond to opportunities, rather than needs. They're often better at recognizing the potential in a project, which is one reason they're wealthy. First-time gifts and recurring, increasing gifts are a sign of a spiritual commitment. A large, one-time gift is more typically a sign of a spiritual response, such as funding a homeless shelter.

There are differing opinions on whether the pastor or chief clergy should know how much individuals give or how much they have. Some clergy and lay people may feel it's an invasion of privacy.

If pastors try to estimate someone's wealth based on appearances, they can be easily deceived. Nice clothes and a fancy car do not mean wealth; they merely indicate a willingness to spend. Real millionaires typically don't look or act the part, so church leaders can only know a person's financial situation by asking. And only by asking can a pastor know whether someone is a great role model of generosity to be emulated, or whether someone is in need of guidance on how to use their assets the way God intended them to be used.

While giving should be personal, it shouldn't necessarily be private. In general, those who most strongly object to any disclosure of their giving are giving at a level they find embarrassing.

We recognize and celebrate acts of kindness in our places of worship, but we tend not to recognize and celebrate acts of generosity, which is merely a subset of kindness. It shouldn't embarrass those who are being recognized; they're being good stewards and role models. It can also serve to encourage others to do more. Their initial motives may be for recognition, but the act of generosity is one of the best ways to create a generous mindset.

Generosity is how we measure our trust in God. If we trust God, we don't worry about money, or at least about being generous with it. If we don't trust God, we look for reasons to *not* be generous, rather than reasons to be generous, which is what God wants for us.

In 1862, during the carnage of the Civil War, the Reverend M.R. Watkinson of Ridleyville, Pennsylvania wrote to Treasury Secretary Salmon P. Chase, urging the U.S. to recognize the deity on its currency. As a result of that request and after much contemplation of the most appropriate way to recognize the Almighty, in 1864 the inscription "In God We Trust" first appeared on our money.

In 1956, in the midst of another war, this time a cold one, as a gesture to distinguish the United States from atheistic communism, Congress passed a joint resolution establishing "In God We Trust" as the official national motto. Since 2001, here in Georgia, that phrase has adorned our state flag, and for the last couple of years, for an extra dollar, you've been able to add it to your license plate.

There are many subjective ways to measure our trust in God, but one of the most objective ways is to look at how we trust God regarding our finances. Specifically, our level of giving is directly correlated with our level of trust in God. The greater the trust, the greater is both our desire and our ability to give, and to give enthusiastically.

The theme of God protecting those who trust in Him is echoed in the book of Jeremiah (17:7-8):

> *"Blessed is the man who trusts in the Lord, whose confidence is in Him. He will be like a tree planted by the water that sends out its roots by the stream. It does not fear when heat comes; its leaves are always green. It has no worries in a year of drought and never fails to bear fruit."*

Paul in Second Corinthians (9:6-8) reminds us of what begets what:

> *"Whoever sows sparingly will also reap sparingly. And whoever sows generously will also reap*

generously. Each man should give what he has decided in his heart to give, not reluctantly or under compulsion, for God loves a cheerful giver."

Among other things, Paul is reminding us that our giving isn't a function of our income. Our income is a function of our giving.

God is constantly reminding us that trusting in Him is not merely the first requirement to personal financial security. God also makes it clear that *only* through trusting in Him can any of us achieve true security, financial or otherwise. This lesson is easier to absorb when we recognize that we're not owners, but merely stewards for God. God trusts us with His entire creation, which also includes all of man's creations, such as money. God trusts us, but He requires trust in return.

When it comes to giving to God, the default method is to subtract our expenses from our income and to give a portion of the remainder. This method has two flaws. First, giving to God is done last, instead of first, as it should be. Second, the remainder, if there's any at all, is usually miniscule.

Giving by gratitude makes giving to God a top priority, though even tithing is based on giving a percentage of income received. Giving by gratitude is better than giving by default, though the element of trust is still lacking. We sow a percentage of what we've already reaped. Even with tithing, we give back one *after* we've received ten.

How would your giving change if you knew that this were the formula: For every dollar you gave to God this year, God would, at some point in the future, give you ten, or fifteen, or even twenty. When it comes to giving, even to God, this approach isn't a comfortable one, although as Christians it should be. Ironically though, we approach investing in this manner. We forego the use of our money in the present, with the hope and expectation, though without guarantee, that we will be rewarded for such sacrifice in the future. Is it really easier to trust in Wall Street than to trust in God?

In sixty-plus years as a Christian and twenty-plus years as a financial planner, I have *never* encountered anyone whose financial situation improved as a result of reduced giving. On the other hand, I've encountered many, many people, myself included, who found that increased giving inevitably brought them an improved financial situation. God is simply the best investment out there. Take it from this expert in the secular alternatives.

Here's what it comes down to – Do you believe that God is so oblivious or indifferent to your situation that He would allow you to be penalized for trusting in Him? That's our belief when we think that we will have less if we give more.

Or do you believe that God, seeing that you've upheld the assertion of trust that's imprinted on every cent you have, would return that trust manifold, not just financially, but also in ways that no amount of money can buy?

RECONCILING SECULAR AND SPIRITUAL

If I say "Star of David", what do you picture? You may picture the flag of Israel in blue and white. You may remember pictures of Jews during World War II who were forced to wear the Star of David to identify themselves as Jews to everyone. You may even picture freemasons or devotees of the occult.

The Star of David is actually a hexagram, a six-pointed geometric star figure, the compound of two equilateral triangles, one pointing up and one pointing down. The intersection is a regular hexagon. ✡

The Star of David is so synonymous with Judaism that we typically refer to it as the Star of David, rather than a hexagram. However, the Star of David didn't emerge as a symbol of Jewish identity until the 19th century, as Jews in Eastern Europe sought a symbol to imitate the influence of the Christian cross. The Star of David was chosen as the central symbol on a flag at the first Zionist Congress in 1897.

The hexagram's history, especially in religion, predates it's fairly recent adoption as a symbol of Judaism. Hexagrams have decorated Christian churches for centuries, including the ceiling of the recently completed National Cathedral in Washington, D.C. Even today, hexagrams can be found in mosques and on other Arabic and Islamic artifacts.

Hexagrams decorate our money, too. If you look on the back of a one-dollar bill, you'll see a hexagram. Above the eagle are thirteen stars, representing the thirteen original states. The stars are arranged to form a hexagram.

Not surprisingly, the oldest known use of hexagrams in religion is in the oldest religion itself, Hinduism. There are different interpretations for what the triangles that comprise the hexagram mean, and even within particular religions there are different and overlapping interpretations of their symbolism. One interpretation that's fairly consistent through time and across different faiths is that the triangle that points down represents God reaching down to us, and the triangle pointing up represents our reaching up to God.

Allow me to add one more interpretation of the hexagram and the triangles comprising it. It's also in conjunction with that last interpretation: the downward pointing triangle is the spiritual world; the upward pointing triangle is the secular world; the hexagon formed where the two triangles overlap is the world in which we live. Our world is one where the spiritual and the secular overlap, where both are in fact necessary for this world to exist.

Albert Einstein, who was at least as wise as he was smart, said, "Science without religion is lame; religion without science is blind." Using Einstein's words to give me a running start, I would add that, where money is involved:

- The secular without the spiritual is *pointless*.
- The spiritual without the secular is *rootless*.

I can't imagine the emptiness and fear that must come over people who, at the end of their lives, realize that they've invested everything in the secular world and nothing in the spiritual world, and they now have to leave behind everything they spent their lives acquiring.

While that realization must be depressing, the terror for me would come when I realized I had an eternity ahead of me for which I hadn't prepared. Secular poverty is a day at the beach compared to spiritual poverty, if for no other reason than secular poverty at least comes with an expiration date.

At age 53, I suffered a heart attack after running a half-marathon in 20-degree weather. (I fully recovered, and I'm wiser for the experience.) There's nothing like a close encounter with the grim reaper to focus one's attention on the truly important things. I made sure I had all my affairs in order, including funeral arrangements. I wrote down some things I hoped people would be able to say about me at my funeral. In reviewing that list, one line is especially relevant here. I hoped people would be able to say that *I was good with money because I knew its limitations as well as its capabilities*.

Most of us don't give enough thought to the limitations of money. We're usually too focused on what we think money could do for us, especially if we won the lottery. But once our time in the secular world is over and the spiritual world is the only one in which we'll dwell, money will become less than irrelevant. You can't take it with you for the simple reason that it has no place where you're going.

In looking over various lists of the most influential people throughout history, it's interesting to see the types of people who make the lists and those who don't. You expect to find great spiritual leaders on these lists, and Jesus, Mohammed, Gandhi, Martin Luther King, Jr., and Mother Teresa are all high up there. Most of the people on the list have made great contributions to the betterment of mankind - people like Einstein, Aristotle, Gutenberg, and Lincoln.

One group that's almost absent from these lists are the wealthy. There are a few people of wealth on these lists – people like Henry Ford and Bill Gates. But this small group consists of people who created something of benefit that happened to make them rich. Well-known billionaires like Warren Buffett or Sam Walton are either well down on these lists or are absent altogether. And no one associated with Wall Street or high finance, even historic figures like J.P. Morgan, is on any of these lists.

Most of us focus on what our resume' says and not enough on what our eulogy will be. On your resume' you list your secular successes. Your eulogy will chronicle what others remember about you, which never includes how much money you made. However, people will pay tribute in your eulogy if you used money to help others.

The lesson here is, if you want to be remembered fondly after you're gone, the way to do it is by improving the quality of others' spiritual or even their secular lives, but certainly not by improving the quality of your own secular life. The secular without the spiritual is pointless.

I enjoy watching TV shows about science and the universe. One reason I enjoy them is the more I learn about the physical world, the more I'm in awe of the God that created it all.

It's hard not to be in awe when you learn that there are hundreds of billions of stars in our galaxy and that there are hundreds of billions of galaxies in the known universe. It's hard not to be in awe when you learn about atoms and how barely a hundred different types of atoms are what everything in the universe is made of, or that all the atoms, including the ones in our bodies, were created some 14 billion years ago. Science doesn't threaten my belief in God; it reinforces it.

The human brain is another of God's most incredible creations. There are at least 100 *trillion* neural connections, or synapses, in the human brain, a number equal to the number of stars in a thousand galaxies. Despite this incredible piece of equipment, humans need help in grasping the spiritual.

When Jesus spoke of God, Heaven, and other spiritual matters, He typically spoke in parables. Jesus knew that, in order for His disciples to begin to comprehend what is otherwise incomprehensible, He had to relate it to things they could comprehend. As a result, many a parable begins, "The Kingdom of Heaven is like…"

In order to give His disciples a chance to comprehend the spiritual, Jesus had to relate it to something in the secular world. I doubt that the secular comparisons Jesus made to Heaven (mustard seeds, treasure buried in fields, etc.) come close to the reality of Heaven, but Jesus had to work with what was available and what His followers could understand. Without something tangible to compare it to, the concepts remained intangible. I feel luckier than the disciples. They had to imagine Heaven from mustard seeds and boxes buried in the ground. I get to imagine it from images of galaxies millions of light years away.

Many of the greatest cathedrals and other houses of worship were built centuries ago, before the Industrial Revolution, before modern construction techniques, and before there was widespread wealth. Why were such sacrifices made to create these places?

If you've ever entered one of the great cathedrals, it's hard not to feel the presence of God in such a place. That feeling is exactly what the creators of these structures were hoping to instill. A cathedral is just a secular building, made of wood and stone and glass and metal. It's subject to the laws of physics and requires maintenance like any other building. However, if it's made magnificent enough, we begin to grasp some of the magnificence of God. After all, if this awesome place is God's house, how awesome must God be?

We all have different secular "wormholes" that enable us to feel a connection to the spiritual. For some, it's a cathedral. For some, it's the beauty of nature demonstrated in a sunset. For me, it's the Mormon Tabernacle Choir singing almost anything. Without the secular, we can't begin to comprehend the spiritual, even with our magnificent brains. The spiritual without the secular is rootless.

I believe the secular world exists for two purposes. First, it exists to supply our physical needs during this phase of our existence. For those with no belief system, that's as far as it goes. However, I believe the more important reason the secular world exists is to give us a way to understand and prepare for the spiritual world that awaits us. If you only believe in the first reason, the secular world has become nothing but a distraction for you. If you also believe in the second reason, the secular world is a roadmap into the spiritual world.

For many, nothing represents the secular world with all its flaws more than money. This belief is formed in large part because they've seen too many cases where money has brought out the worst in people. Money certainly has that ability, but money is a mirror. Money has no qualities of its own; it simply reflects the qualities of those who possess it, bad and good.

If you want people to become less secular and more spiritual, one of the best places to begin transformation is through their use of money. Even if the goal is simply to help people better understand the roles of the secular and the spiritual, money is a useful tool for that purpose.

Think about the properties of money. It incorporates many of the characteristics of the secular and the spiritual. You can see it and touch it. You can even roll around in it if you have enough of it. Money, as represented by currency, definitely feels secular.

Money is precise and measurable. One of the most important characteristics of money is our ability to know exactly how much of it we have at any particular moment. Whether it's the currency in your wallet or the value of your 401(k), money is very secular in the ability to know its precise quantity.

Almost anything in the secular world can be attained with a sufficient amount of money. If we had to pick one thing to represent the secular world, money would be an excellent choice. Because money can bring out the worst in some people, it can also represent the worst of our secular selves.

Money also mimics characteristics of the spiritual. Money is only of value to those who believe in its value. Once the Confederacy was defeated in the Civil War, Confederate money became worthless because no one believed in its value any longer. Those who don't believe in the spiritual believe it's of no value to believe. They view spirituality as something counterfeit. Money, like God, does require a certain element of faith in it.

Money can bring out the worst in our secular selves, but it can also reveal the best of our spiritual side. Every time we use money to benefit others, we reveal our spirituality. When you think of the countless ways you can do God's will, money can assist you in doing God's will more than anything else that exists in the secular world.

Money has the ability to reflect more of our secular and spiritual natures than anything else on our planet. Money not only works well in both of these worlds, but it also has a unique ability to work between the secular and the spiritual, to bridge the gap between them, and to reconcile the two to each other.

If there's someone in need, our money can help that person, like the Good Samaritan's money helped him to care for the man who was robbed and beaten. We can turn greed into generosity by simply turning money from an inward to an outward direction. Money can finance the mission work of people donating their time and talent, but who still have to obtain material goods in the secular world.

Money is limited in its ability to reconcile the secular and the spiritual only by our imagination and by our willingness to use money in that manner. Remember, money is amoral – it merely reflects the morality or immorality of the one using it. If you want to make the world a better place, if you want people, including yourself, to become more spiritual and less secular, if you simply want harmony between your secular and spiritual halves, start by thinking of how money can take part in making those changes. You'll be surprised how accommodating money can be to such ends.

Idolatry is being possessed by a possession. It causes one to refuse God's claim on oneself and to shirk one's responsibility to others in the community. Economy, sexuality, and knowledge are the chief fields in which idolatry takes place. In these areas we're most prone to claim self-sufficiency and the power to subjugate our environment, other persons, and even our own bodies. Sexuality and knowledge have large, but limited, numbers of subjects, but money is something everyone wants and needs to some degree. No one is totally immune from the temptation to idolize money.

Money was never created to be an object of idolatry. It was created for a noble purpose. Money is an inspired invention of people who understood the play of forces in human life. It was created as a way of recognizing that humans have property rights, but that no human is self-sufficient. Money was created to help maintain a relationship between man's spiritual needs and his material needs. Money was created to harmonize the disparate elements of the secular and the spiritual. Money was created to be a tool of reconciliation.

Money's most important function is as a tool of reconciliation and enlightenment. The key to better understanding your secular and spiritual worlds and to reconciling the two is not to ignore or condemn money. The key is to get *closer* to money, to understand it fully, to learn its capabilities and its limitations. Such understanding transcends knowledge and becomes wisdom. The people in this world who have the most harmonious balance of the secular and the spiritual are the people who make the effort to *know* money.

MISCELLANEOUS MONEY MUSINGS

The possession of gold has ruined fewer men than the lack of it.

-Thomas Bailey Aldrich

If God would only give me some clear sign! Like making a deposit in my name in a Swiss bank account.

-Woody Allen

Work for your future as if you are going to live forever, for your afterlife as if you are going to die tomorrow.

-Arabian Proverb

One cannot both feast and become rich.

-Ashanti Proverb

Riches are a good handmaid, but the worst mistress.

-Sir Francis Bacon

Money is a terrible master but an excellent servant.

-P.T. Barnum

The true way to gain much is never desire to gain too much. He is not rich that possesses much, but he that covets no more; and he is not poor that enjoys little, but he that wants too much.

-Francis Beaumont

Interest works day and night in fair weather and in foul. It gnaws at a man's substance with invisible teeth.

-Henry Ward Beecher

If any man is rich and powerful, he comes under the law of God by which the higher branches must take the burning of the sun and shade those that are lower; the tall trees must protect the weak plants beneath them.

-Henry Ward Beecher

If you want to know how rich you really are, find out what would be left of you tomorrow if you should lose every dollar you own tonight.

-William Boetcker

Frugality is founded on the principle that all riches have limits.

-Edmund Burke

Cessation of work is not accompanied by cessation of expenses.

-Cato the Elder

The gratification of wealth is not found in mere possession or in lavish expenditure, but in its wise application.

-Miguel de Cervantes

Never stand begging for that which you have the power to earn.

-Miguel de Cervantes

Riches should be admitted into our houses, but not into our hearts; we may take them into our possession, but not into our affections.

-Pierre Charron

We make a living by what we get; we make a life by what we give.

-Winston Churchill

If you mean to profit, learn to please.

-Winston Churchill

It is difficult to set bounds to the price unless you first set bounds to the wish.

-Cicero

Frugality includes all the other virtues.

-Cicero

He who will not economize will have to agonize.

-Confucius

In a country well governed, poverty is something to be ashamed of. In a country badly governed, wealth is something to be ashamed of.

-Confucius

When prosperity comes, do not use all of it.

-Confucius

There is no dignity quite so impressive and no independence quite so important as living within your means.

-Calvin Coolidge

Prosperity is only an instrument to be used, not a deity to be worshipped.

-Calvin Coolidge

With money you can buy:
a house…but not a home; a clock…but not time
a bed…but not sleep; a book…but not knowledge
medicine…but not health; position…but not respect
blood…but not life; sex…but not love.

-Chinese Proverb

Thousands upon thousands are yearly brought into a state of real poverty by their great anxiety not to be thought poor.

-William Corbett

Plan ahead; it wasn't raining when Noah built the ark.

-Bishop Richard Cushing

In prosperity, caution; in adversity, patience.

-Dutch Proverb

Not everything that can be counted counts. And not everything that counts can be counted.

-Albert Einstein

Sometimes one pays most for the things one gets for nothing.

-Albert Einstein

The first wealth is health.

-Ralph Waldo Emerson

Economy does not consist in saving the coal, but in using the time while it burns.

-Ralph Waldo Emerson

Poor men seek meat for their stomachs; rich men seek stomachs for their meat.

-English Proverb

The man least indebted to tomorrow meets tomorrow most cheerfully.

-Epicurus

If we don't discipline ourselves, the world will do it for us.

-William Feather

Mankind, by the perverse depravity of their nature, esteem that which they have most desired as of no value the moment it is possessed, and torment themselves with fruitless wishes for that which is beyond their reach.

-Francois Fenelon

No amount of money is worth the sacrifice of one's better instincts, of one's self-respect – of one's soul, if you wish. Riches not gained legitimately and decently are not worth having.

-B.C. Forbes

Too many people overvalue what they are not and undervalue what they are.

-Malcolm Forbes

What maintains one vice would bring up two children.

-Benjamin Franklin

God helps them that help themselves.

-Benjamin Franklin

Contentment makes poor men rich; discontent makes rich men poor.

-Benjamin Franklin

Who is rich? He that rejoices in his portion.

-Benjamin Franklin

It is only when the rich are sick that they fully feel the impotence of wealth.

-Benjamin Franklin

Earth provides enough to satisfy every man's need, but not every man's greed.

-Mahatma Gandhi

God provides the nuts, but He does not crack them.

-German Proverb

Is not dread of thirst when your well is full the thirst that is unquenchable?

-Kahlil Gibran

Money is like love; it kills slowly and painfully the one who withholds it, and it enlivens the one who turns it upon his fellow man.

-Kahlil Gibran

I am indeed rich, since my income is superior to my expense, and my expense is equal to my wishes.

-Edward Gibson

This is one of the bitter curses of poverty: it leaves no right to be generous.

-George Gissing

The darkest hour of any man's life is when he sits down to plan how to get money without earning it.

-Horace Greeley

Leave the woodpile higher than you found it.

-Paul Harvey

A gift much expected is paid, not given.

-George Herbert

Failure can be bought on easy terms; success must be paid for in advance.

-Cullen Hightower

The future is purchased by the present.

-Samuel Johnson

A decent provision for the poor is the true test of civilization.

-Samuel Johnson

The chains of habit are too weak to be felt until they are too strong to be broken.

-Samuel Johnson

All the money in the world is no use to a man or his country if he spends it as fast as he makes it. All he has left is his bills and the reputation for being a fool.

-Rudyard Kipling

No gain is as certain as that which proceeds from the economical use of what you already have.

-Latin Proverb

That some should be rich shows that others may become rich and, hence, is just encouragement to industry and enterprise. Let not he who is houseless pull down the house of another, but let him labor diligently and build one for himself, thus, by example, assuring that his own shall be safe from violence when built.

-Abraham Lincoln

Any society that takes away from those most capable and gives to the least will perish.

-Abraham Lincoln

I don't like money actually, but it quiets my nerves.

-Joe Louis

That money is where most of us are tested says precisely as much about the weakness of man as it does about the power of money.

-Jacob Needleman

I would rather have people laugh at my economies than weep for my extravagance.

-King Oscar II of Sweden

You should always love people and use money, rather than the reverse.

-Bob Proctor

To be without some of the things you want is an indispensable part of happiness.

-Bertrand Russell

A goal without a plan is just a wish.

-Antoine de Saint-Exupery

Ask thy purse what thou should spend.

-Scottish Proverb

No one can be poor who has enough, nor rich who covets more.

-Seneca

A great fortune is a great slavery.

-Seneca

Neither a borrower nor a lender be.
For loan oft loses both itself and friend,
And borrowing dulls the edge of husbandry.

-William Shakespeare

It is the mind that makes the body rich.

-William Shakespeare

Never measure your generosity by what you give, but rather by what you have left.

-Bishop Fulton J. Sheen

Those who obtain riches by labor, care, and watching know their value. Those who impart them to sustain knowledge, virtue, and religion know their use. Those who lose them by accident or fraud know their vanity. And those who experience the difficulties and dangers of preserving them know their perplexities.

-Charles Simmons

Virtue is not given by money, but that from virtue comes money and every other good of man.

-Socrates

A wise man should have money in his head, but not in his heart.

-Jonathan Swift

There must be a reason why some people can afford to live well. They must have worked for it. I only feel angry when I see waste; when I see people throwing away things we could use.

-Mother Teresa

No one would remember the Good Samaritan if he'd only had good intentions. He had money, too.

-Margaret Thatcher

A man is rich in proportion to the things he can afford to let alone.

-Henry David Thoreau

Money is not required to buy one necessity of the soul.

-Henry David Thoreau

Money is a new form of slavery, which differs from the old only in being impersonal, and in freeing people from all the human relations of the slave.

-Leo Tolstoy

Worldly riches are like nuts; many clothes are torn getting them, many a tooth broke in cracking them, but never a belly full in eating them.

-Ralph Venning

He who wishes to be rich in a day will be hanged in a year.

-Leonardo da Vinci

Hell is the state in which we are barred from receiving what we truly need because of the value we give to what we merely want.

-Virgil

Happy the man who has learned the cause of things and has put under his feet all fear, inexorable fate, and the noisy strife of the hell of greed.

-Virgil

Work banishes those three great evils, boredom, vice and poverty.

-Voltaire

Make all you can, save all you can, give all you can.

-John Wesley

Before enlightenment, you chop wood and carry water. After enlightenment, you chop wood and carry water.

-Zen Proverb

REFERENCES

Ariely, Dan; *Predictably Irrational*; 2008; Harper Collins

Ariely, Dan; *The Honest Truth about Dishonesty*; 2012; Harper Collins

Ariely, Dan; *The Upside of Irrationality*; 2010; Harper Collins

Bailey, Joseph; *Fearproof Your Life*: 2007; Conari Press

Baumeister, Roy F. & Tierney, John; *Willpower*; 2011; Penguin Press

Belsky, Gary and Gilovich, Thomas: *Why Smart People Make Big Money Mistakes*; 1999; Simon and Shuster

Bogle, John C.; *Enough*; 2009; John Wiley and Sons

Brafman, Ori and Brafman, Ron; *Sway*; 2008; Doubleday

Chabris, Christopher & Simons, Daniel; *The Invisible Gorilla*; 2010; Crown

Clason, George; *The Richest Man in Babylon;* 1926; Signet Press

Davies, Glyn; *A History of Money from Ancient Times to the Present Day;* 2002; University of Wales Press

DeGraff, John, et al; *Affluenza*; 2005; Berrett Koehler

Duhigg, Charles; *The Power of Habit*; 2012; Random House

Dungan, Nathan; *Speaking of Faith: Money and Moral Balance*; 2004

Easterbrook, Gregg; *The Progress Paradox*; 2003; Random House

Eisenberg, Lee; *The Number*; 2006; Free Press

Frankl, Viktor; *Man's Search for Meaning*; 1959; Beacon Press

Frederickson, Barbara L.; *The Value of Positive Emotions*; 2003; *American Scientist*

Friedman, Milton; *Free to Choose*; 1980; Harcourt Press

Gardner, Daniel; *The Science of Fear*; 2008; Dutton

Gladwell, Malcolm; *The Tipping Point*; 2000; Little, Brown, & Co.

Goetz, David L.; *Death by Suburb*; 2006; Harper Collins

Haidt, Jonathan; *The Happiness Hypothesis*; 2006; Basic Books

Halpern, David; *The Hidden Wealth of Nations*; 2010; Polity Press

Harford, Tim; *Adapt*; 2011; Farrar, Straus and Giroux

Harford, Tim; *The Logic of Life*; 2008; Random House

Heath, Chip & Heath, Dan; *Switch*; 2011; Broadway Books

Iyengar, Sheena; *The Art of Choosing*; 2011; Twelve Publishing

James, William; *The Principles of Psychology*; 1890, 1950; Dover Publications

Kahneman, Daniel; *Thinking, Fast and Slow*; 2011; Farrar, Straus and Giroux

Kasser, Tim; *The High Price of Materialism*; 2002; MIT Press

Katz, Aya; *Avarice vs. Greed*; 2008

Keller, Timothy; *Counterfeit Gods*; 2009; Dutton

Kidder, Rushworth; *How Good People Make Tough Choices*; 1995; Harper Collins

Kinder, George; *The Seven Stages of Money Maturity*; 1999; Delacorte Press

Koch, Richard; *The 80/20 Principle*; 1998; Currency

Lehrer, Jonah; *Don't!*; 5/18/2009; *The New Yorker*;

Lewis, Michael; *Boomerang*; 2011; W.W. Norton

Lupton, Robert D.; *Toxic Charity*; 2010; Harper One

Lyubomirsky, Sonja; *The How of Happiness*; 2007; Penguin Press

Manning, Robert D.; *Credit Card Nation*; 2000; Basic Books

Maslow, A.; *Motivation and Personality;* 1970; Harper and Row

Mauboussin, Michael J.; *More Than You Know*; 2008; Columbia University Press

Meeks, M. Douglas; God the Economist; 1989; Fortress Press

Moody, Harry R.; *The Five Stages of the Soul*; 1997; Anchor

Morgenson, Gretchen & Rosner, Joshua; *Reckless Endangerment*; 2011; Times Books

Murray, Nick; *The Excellent Investment Advisor*; 1996

Needleman, Jacob; *Money and the Meaning of Life*; 1991; Doubleday

Nietzsche, Friedrich; *Beyond Good and Evil*; 1886

Pink, Daniel H.; *A Whole New Mind*; 2006; Berkley Publishing Group

Pink, Daniel H.; *Drive*; 2009; Riverhead Books

Piquet, Howard; *The Economic Axioms*; Vantage Press; 1978

Pizzigati, Sam; *Greed and Good*; 2004; Apex Press

Richards, Jay W.; *Money, Greed and God*; 2009; Harper Collins

Ridley, Matt; *The Rational Optimist*; 2010; Harper Collins

Riley, Jason L.; *Please Stop Helping Us*; 2014; Encounter Books

Sadler, William A.; *The Third Age*; 2000; Da Capo Press

Sadler, William A. & Krefft, James H.; *Changing Course*; 2007; Center for Third Age leadership

Schor, Juliet; *Born to Buy*; 2004; Scribner

Schor, Juliet; *The Overspent American*; 1998; Harper Perennial

Schwartz, Barry; *The Paradox of Choice*; 2004; Harper Collins

Shefrin, Hersh; *Beyond Greed and Fear*; 2002; Oxford University Press

Simmel, George; *The Philosophy of Money*; 1978; Routledge

Sinek, Simon; *Start with Why*; 2009; Portfolio/Penguin

Skinner, B.F.; *Science and Human Behavior*; 1964; Free Press

Sowell, Thomas; *Basic Economics – A Citizen's Guide to the Economy*; Basic Books; 2004

Stanley, Thomas & Danko, William; *The Millionaire Next Door*; 1996; Pocket Books

Statman, Meir; *What Investors Really Want*; 2011; McGraw Hill

Taleb, Nassim Nicholas; *The Black Swan*; 2007; Random House

Tawney, R.H.; *The Acquisitive Society*; 1920; Harcourt, Brace, & Howe

Thaler, Richard H. & Sunstein, Cass R.; *Nudge*; 2008; Yale University Press

Weatherford, Jack; *The History of Money*; 1997; Three Rivers Press

Whybrow, Peter C.; *American Mania*; 2005; W.W. Norton

Willard, Chris & Sheppard, Jim; *Contagious Generosity*; 2012; Zondervan

Zeldin, Theodore; *An Intimate History of Humanity*; 1994; Harper Perennial

WEB SITES

123helpme.com
30-days.net
aish.com
authentichappiness.org
bbc.co.uk
berkeleycenter.georgetown.edu
buddhism.about.com
budsas.org
centurionministry.org
christianpf.com
economist.com

effectiveislamicparenting.com
examiner.com
finerminds.com
hindism.co.za
hinduism.about.com
hinduismtoday.com
hubpages.com
humanmetrics.com
knowledge.wharton.upenn.edu
illuminatedmind.net
islamreligion.com
kiva.org
myersbriggs.org
newadvent.org
nytimes.com
philanthropy.com
projects.exeter.ac.uk
psychologytoday.com
religionfacts.com
sciencedaily.com
sidsavara.com
thestreet.com
time.com
virtuesproject.com
whitestonejournal.com
wikipedia.org
wildmind.org
zakat.org

Mark DiGiovanni is founder and president of Marathon Financial Strategies in Atlanta, Georgia. The name of the firm comes from a lifetime of running and Mark's belief that achieving financial goals requires the same persistence and discipline as running a marathon.

Mark was one of the first seven CFP Ambassadors appointed by the Certified Financial Planner Board of Standards. In this role, he supports the CFP Board's Consumer Advocacy Program and addresses the financial issues of the American consumer through public speaking engagements and media appearances.

Mark's professional mission is to:

ENLIGHTEN - Helping people understand their Life's Missions, leading to understanding the *why* as well as the *what* of their financial goals, desires, and fears;

ENABLE - Solving problems and removing barriers that prevent people from achieving their Life's Missions;

ENRICH – The purpose of wealth is to serve as a tool to help people achieve their Life's Missions. It isn't the number of tools, but their skillful use, that determines success.

You can learn more about Mark DiGiovanni at www.marathon-forthelongrun.com.
Contact him at mark@marathon-forthelongrun.com.